THE OAKWOOD PRESS

A
History of Slipping
and
Slip Carriages

by
C.E.J. Fryer

THE OAKWOOD PRESS

© Oakwood Press and C.E.J. Fryer 1997

British Library Cataloguing in Publication Data
A Record for this book is available from the British Library
ISBN 0 85361 514 4

Typeset by Oakwood Graphics.
Repro by Ford Graphics, Ringwood, Hants.
Printed by Alpha Print (Oxford) Ltd, Witney, Oxon.

Dedication

To all my friends in the Republic of Ireland.

Slip portion of mail vans detached from the GWR's Plymouth-London Ocean Mail special near Bristol *c*. 1905. Note the special Post Office vestibule connection - so arranged in order that it could not be connected to any ordinary train. *Railway Magazine*

Published by
The Oakwood Press
P.O. Box 122, Headington, Oxford, OX3 8LU.

Contents

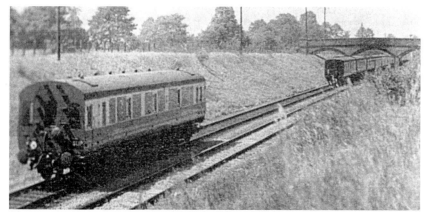

The Weymouth slip from the 'Cornish Riviera Express' being made just before Heywood Road Junction, Westbury. *Author's Collection*

Introduction

Now, more than 35 years since the last coach was slipped from the rear of a British main line railway train, it is surely time for some connected account to be written about this century-long phenomenon, before records of its use and frequency vanish from libraries and archives as the paper on which they were printed crumbles away. One essential source of information is the published timetables of railways, whose earliest copies are now beginning to moulder. Even the British Library no longer has copies of Bradshaw's Guide in unbroken sequence right back to the beginning, and it is too much to expect that those which do remain should be put on microfilm at great expense and potted instead of being put on shelves, there to blush unseen (if the metaphor be not inapt) since few would ever want to consult them. I am thankful for the help of those who have enabled me to consult such old records, and acknowledge especially those publishers who have ventured to reproduce facsimile copies of some old timetables.

I am also much indebted to writers of articles in magazines and journals, most of them from earlier days, but in particular a recent one on Irish Slip Services by Dr D.B. McNeill, published in the Journal of the Irish Railway Record Society. As to unpublished material, I am especially grateful for having been given a sight of typescripts of talks given to the Railway Club by the late G.W.T. Daniel in 1934 and the late Canon R.B. Fellows in 1941. I am much indebted, too, to Mr B.D.J. Walsh, who drew my attention to both of these and also lent me a copy of the script of a talk he himself gave to the Great Eastern Railway Society in 1992. I must also acknowledge in particular the contribution made by the late M.W. Earley, whose superb photographs have graced so many pages of past books and railway journals, who at some point after the formation of British Railways made a sequence of seven pictures illustrating a slip made at Reading from an up express from the West Country, copies of which feature in this book. Finally I must include a word of appreciation to Mr R.W. Kidner, who read the first draft of this book and made some very useful suggestions and corrections.

I lay no claim to being comprehensive. No doubt many items of information, buried in the columns of past journals or pigeonholed in archives, have been omitted through ignorance. I have not included, either, details of slips made experimentally in other countries, particularly France and Holland, for short periods during the later 19th and earlier 20th centuries. My aim has been to present an overall picture of slipping in Britain and Ireland, and some of the nuts and bolts may not be showing.

This book is of course concerned with slipping operations approved by the railway companies concerned; however, I have included in Appendix One, more for amusement than information, an account of personal enterprise on the part of the late Victorian philosopher Herbert Spencer, who unofficially carried out what must surely have been the first slip of any kind on a British line, when he was a young man working as an employee on the still-unfinished London and Birmingham Railway, to which he confessed in his posthumously-published autobiography, written in his old age and published in 1904.

Chapter One

Slip Coach Beginnings: 1858

There was a story, long current among railwaymen though never officially confirmed, that the practice of slipping carriages from trains in rapid motion originated by accident. It was said that on a certain occasion in the early days of rail travel, before continuous brakes would have ensured that a train which broke apart would at once start to slow down and eventually come to a halt, a highly-placed railway official, wishing to travel from a terminal station to an intermediate one, mistakenly boarded, on the wrong side of a departure platform, a train due to run a considerable distance before its first booked stop. He discovered his mistake when the train ran through one of the stations at which he had expected it to stop, and resigned himself at having to alight beyond his intended destination and then retrace his journey. His surprise was great, therefore, when the coach he was in began to slow down on approaching the station where he had meant to alight, and eventually came to a halt at the platform.

His astonishment was even greater when, having stepped out of his compartment, he saw the front part of the train disappearing into the distance while its last coach, in which he had travelled, was standing alone at the platform. A few words with the train's guard, who had also been travelling in it, explained the situation. The coupling had snapped, and the guard, using his wits and realising that they were then near enough to a station to coast into it by their own momentum, had braked the carriage gradually to a halt at the platform. The driver of the locomotive was still unaware of what had happened, for the alarm cord that ran along the side of the train had snapped when the coupling did, so that the alarm bell on the tender had either failed to sound or had rung only momentarily and had not been noticed. No doubt some signalman, noticing the absence of a tail light on what remained of the train, eventually would have halted it by notifying the next signal box by telegraph.

The consequence, according to the story, was that the official concerned began to reflect on the possibility of making such a convenient accident a matter of deliberate controlled practice, and made suggestions at a high level, which resulted in the slipping of coaches becoming a regular thing. It is perhaps a matter for surprise that an event which reflected no discredit on anyone at all (except the manufacturers of the snapped coupling) should never have been officially admitted, and this may indicate that the incident was not real but *ben trovato*. If the story *is* true, the London, Brighton & South Coast Railway (LB&SCR), on which the first advertised slip took place, could well have been the line on which the event occurred. Imagination toys with the idea of some top-hatted gentleman boarding a train at Brighton terminus and turning right into a train which was due to stop first at (say) Redhill or East Croydon instead of left into an all-stations train due to halt at (say) Haywards Heath, where he had intended to alight.

Precedents for slipping carriages from slow-moving trains had in fact already been set in East London and West Cornwall. In 1840 the London and Blackwall Railway was opened, and for several years was cable-operated by wire ropes wound on and off drums. Its trains were composed of seven 6-wheeled carriages, five of which were slipped singly from the rear at each of the five intermediate stations, only the first two reaching the terminus. However, the system kept breaking down, and in 1849 steam locomotives replaced cable haulage.

Meanwhile on the Hayle Railway a regular service had operated since 1843 for passengers, whose coaches were attached to the rear of a mineral train which ran from Redruth to a quayside at Hayle, on a route which was later incorporated into the Great Western Railway's main line to Penzance. In its earlier days no high speeds had been attempted on this line, so the practice about to be described was perhaps less risky than it sounds. As the mixed train drew near to Hayle the guard in charge of the wagons would unhook the passenger vehicles, which began to slow down. The wagons, proceeding ahead of them, ran through points which led to the right towards the quayside; the passenger vehicles, rolling more slowly, but not usually actually coming to a stand, were quickly attached to a waiting horse and drawn into the station. There was one occasion, however, when matters went awry and the wagons became derailed short of the junction, so that the already-detached passenger vehicles ran into the back of them. Nobody was seriously hurt, but the happening was reported in the local press; it is mentioned here because it prefigures the only kind of accident that ever happened to slip coaches in later days. It does not seem to have prevented the continuation of the practice at Hayle.

In February 1858, when John Chester Craven was in charge of the Locomotive, Carriage and Wagon Department at Brighton, and presumably approved the experiment, the 4 pm from London Bridge to Brighton, non-stop to the latter from East Croydon, began the practice of slipping a portion at Haywards Heath for Lewes and Hastings.*   A working timetable for the LB&SCR for that month carried the following special direction for those railway servants concerned in the operation:

> On leaving London Bridge, the Brighton part of the train will be in front. Each part will have two guards and two tail lights, so that when detached at Haywards Heath each part will form a perfectly-appointed train.
> Before leaving London Bridge the Head Guard of the Hastings part must see that it is properly coupled with the patent coupling, and that the side chains are not coupled but hung up. He must also see that his rope connection with the Brighton under-guard is properly connected.
> On arriving near the Haywards Heath distant signal, the speed being considerably slackened, the Head Guard of the Hastings part will first detach his rope communication from the Brighton train, then his coupling, seeing which properly effected, the under-guard of the Brighton train will give his hand signal to the driver to proceed. The Head Guard of the Hastings train will then brake it gently, and not too suddenly, up to the station platform.
> In case anything should prevent the detaching, the guards must give a stop signal to the driver, who must then stop at the station.

---

* There is, however, a possibility that the South Eastern Railway was making slips a month earlier: See Appendix Four.

If by any chance the train should become detached before arriving at the proper place, the snapping asunder of the guard's and driver's communicator will warn them all of the occurrence, and they must act in accordance with General Rules 43 and 173.

The under-guard of the Hastings train will leave the braking of it at Haywards Heath to the Head Guard, and must only give his assistance if necessary.

Care must be taken at London Bridge to prevent passengers for Haywards Heath or East Branch [i.e. the Lewes and Hastings branch] from getting into the Brighton part of the train.

The Hastings engine must not leave the siding at Haywards Heath until the train has actually stopped at the platform.

Some comments seem called for. It has to be borne in mind that the vehicles were four- or six-wheeled coaches with no continuous brakes, and linked together not only by couplings but also by side chains which gave some added stability while running. The rope was a stout cord which ran the length of the train outside and above the windows, attached at the front to a bell or whistle on the locomotive, and at the other end to a bell in the guard's van, which was necessarily therefore the last vehicle in the train. When pulled in an emergency it warned both driver and guard that the train had to stop. But when coaches were slipped the engine, though it might (as instructed here) require to be slowed down, did not stop. So the rope had to be disconnected between the rear of the main train and the front of the slip portion. This was all that was necessary before the Head Guard effected the slip.

The latter operation was evidently performed by using the patent coupling, which appears to have been a device in which the link opened when an obstruction was removed by pulling on a rope fixed to the link's lower end and reachable by the guard at the upper end. No details of the actual device used on this railway appear to have survived, but it may not have been so very different from that used on the London and South Western Railway at the end of the century, which is described and sketched in Chapter Six. Finally, the Head Guard, controlling the handbrake in his compartment, brought the slipped coach to a halt at the platform. Shortly afterwards it proceeded to Hastings behind another locomotive, diverging from the main line at Keymer Junction. The reason why the Hastings-bound locomotive was prohibited from moving out of its siding until the detached coach had come to rest was presumably in case, if the brakes on the slip coach had failed to act properly, the latter might have collided with it.

All this was before the introduction of continuous braking by vacuum or compressed air equipment. Steam heating of carriages from the locomotive boiler was also not yet practised. Therefore there was no need to disconnect any piping, which was convenient; less convenient was the fact that the slip guard had only his hand brake to rely upon in order to bring the coach to a halt at the station platform.

In the same year two other companies began slipping coaches - or perhaps one should say that one certainly, the other probably did. The probable example was on the South Eastern Railway, from the 12.30 pm from London Bridge to Ramsgate, which was routed through Tonbridge and Ashford. It had no booked stop between Ashford and Ramsgate, but included a portion for

Canterbury. A notice in the *Kentish Gazette* informed the public that the train was 'first class from London to Ramsgate and Margate, and second class to Canterbury, where the carriages are detached; the train does not call there.' This probably *was* a slip service, but the arrangement could conceivably have been that the train halted momentarily outside Canterbury while the coupling was unhooked and then proceeded on its way.

Later in the year the Great Western first experimented with and then introduced a slip carriage service. The experiment was made at Slough on the 5.10 pm from Paddington, the method used not being recorded. This was in November; a month later it was announced in the GWR public timetable that 'a carriage would be detached for Banbury' from the 9.30 am express from Paddington to Birmingham. This was certainly a genuine case of slipping, since a notice in the *Banbury Advertiser*, referring to this train, makes mention of a carriage 'being here detached from the express down train without the train slackening speed.' The GWR's historian, E.T. MacDermot, records that the slip guard pulled a rope attached to the coupling but no other details are available. There were occasions later when the slip portion broke away from the main train, and official opinion was that this was due to a weakness in 'the spring which confines the slip catch between the slip carriages and the main train.'

Seven years later the GWR issued a circular notice to those of its employees who were concerned, containing this instruction:

> The guard in charge of the slip coach must be careful to see, before starting, that the slip connection is in good working order and free from grit or dirt, and also that it is properly fixed for slipping . . . When slipping the coach, immediately the connection is let go he must apply his brake as hard as he can in order to let the train get well ahead of the slip coach . . . As soon as he has got his carriage a sufficient distance from the train and well under control he will ease off the brake and let the carriage run slowly into the station. The carriage should never be allowed to run into the station at any considerable speed.

If for any reason he failed to detach his coach he had to signal to the head guard of the main train 'by means of a red flag by day or a red lamp by night, waved on the off-side of the train.' His counterpart on the main train had to be on the look-out for such signals, and the slip guard, if he failed the first time to effect the detachment, was not to make a second attempt but had to signal and then wait for the whole train to come to a halt at the platform.

Once slipping had begun on the railways mentioned above, the idea caught hold of the public imagination, and many people made suggestions or indulged in speculations, both in Great Britain and on the Continent. One may perhaps mention a fantastic proposal by a French engineer, M. Guichard Petrus, reported in the English *Times* on 30th November, 1858, in which special machinery was required

> . . . for lifting one carriage off and for placing another carriage on a train while in motion. His invention required the use of a corridored train, so that passengers could get to and from the last carriage, the body of which was detachable from the frame and could be lifted off at a station while the train was in motion, and another coach body, holding

passengers from the station, could be lifted on. The lifting was to be done by machinery placed on the edge of the railway. The apparatus would grasp the body of the last coach and transfer it to the ground, and another machine further on would place the body of a carriage containing the passengers on to the empty framework at the end of the still-moving train.

Herapath's Railway and Commercial Journal of 11th December, 1858, in a leading article on 'Railway Novelties', refers to M. Petrus' proposal and concludes:

If an experiment of this kind should ever be attempted, we hope the inventor will not fail to be one of the party to be caught up, but before he do so, let him make his will and take leave of his friends.

Assuming that the Frenchman's proposal was intended to be taken seriously, and was not just a piece of Gallic fun at the expense of supposed English stupidity (it was, after all, not very long since the Charge of the Light Brigade), two obvious objections arise. How was the detachable coach body to be transferred to its carrying truck at exactly the right moment if, as one supposes, the lifting mechanism were stationary at the lineside? It would need to wait until the whole train had reached a certain point, and then position the coach body on its moving base in a fraction of a second. The mind boggles at the thought of how such an operation could be so rapidly accomplished even if the carriage only contained inanimate materials. Furthermore, if it contained people, how were these to be cushioned against the sudden shock of acceleration in a split second from 0 to (say) 20 mph? Equally, in the case of a coach to be removed from the train, which would in effect come suddenly to a dead stand, what would happen to the people in it? The only conceivable mitigating device, which would have allowed both the taking-off and the placing-on mechanisms to operate without sudden jolts, would have been for each to be in wheels on a long siding parallel to the line, and to be itself mobile, so that when the train was approaching it could set off in the same direction and run alongside it at the same speed for some distance. At least half a mile of track would be needed for such an operation, together with an attached locomotive capable of matching the speed of the train, and kept continuously in steam. The whole concept seems analogous to using a steam hammer to crack a nut.

In 1860 a certain John Cooper patented a method for having the rear vehicle in a vestibuled train detachable. Before the slipping point was reached, all persons wishing to alight at the destined station were to go back along the train to the carriage in question, whose corridor connection would then be sealed off; the coupling would then be loosened. Mr Cooper also proposed a method for attaching a coach to a train in motion. The former would be standing in a siding parallel to the main line. As the rear end of the moving train passed the stationary coach, a hook upon the former would catch the end of a rope suspended from a sliding pole upon the latter, and the train would catch its additional burden in somewhat the same way as an angler catches a fish. Once the passengers had recovered from the shock of being so rapidly put into motion, a further shock would await them as their coach was suddenly pulled sideways in behind the main train when the points joining the siding to the main line were reached. One cannot suppose that Mr Cooper's patent brought him any royalties.

Such suggestions, from the wilder shores of misplaced ingenuity or bizarre humour were never, so far as one knows, tried out. Railway companies, however, once slipping had become an established practice, did ponder on the possibilities of attaching carriages to trains in motion, but no method was ever discovered that seemed either safe or suitable.

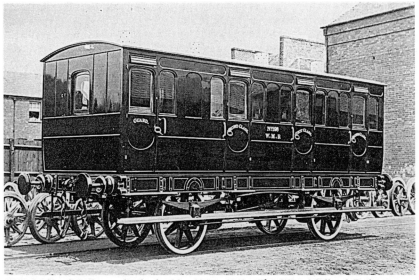

West Midland Railway slip brake No. 196 c. 1860. The West Midland Railway was absorbed into the GWR in 1863. This vehicle was built by the Gloucester Carriage & Wagon Co.   *HMRS*

Chapter Two

The Build-Up:
1859-1900

Following the three pioneers of 1858, most of the other British railway companies adopted the practice with varying degrees of enthusiasm; the adjacent diagram shows how it rose or fell during the last quarter of the 19th century. It will be observed that there was no universal trend towards a greater use of slipping. Some lines showed a steady increase in its daily incidence - the Great Western in particular; some made a big thing of it at first but then apparently became unsure of its usefulness and lessened its employment; some made only slight or moderate use of it; some fought shy entirely and are not shown on the diagram. Evidently the Boards of different companies judged differently at different times as to whether it was financially advantageous.

The GWR, which had been the third to adopt the practice, added to its daily totals, with one slight temporary decrease, over the whole period, and soon took the lead. Most were from down trains at Slough, the slipped portions going on to Windsor; earlier there had been as many as 10 daily in some years, the figure settling down eventually to a steady five, six or seven. On this service a slip portion could be used as much as three times daily, working back to Paddington as an ordinary composite coach before being re-marshalled at the rear of another train in order to be slipped once more. One curious feature of the Paddington-Windsor service was a slip from an up train near Paddington *for* Paddington, which operated from the summer of 1866 for two years. The 8.15 from Windsor, routed to the City by way of Bishop's Road, Paddington on the Metropolitan line, slipped a coach with a luggage compartment at Westbourne Bridge; after coming to a halt it was drawn into the main terminus by another engine.

The use of the same coach more than once daily could not have been so easily managed with slips much further away from London, such as those at Didcot or Chippenham, but at these places, too, one sees a slow increase in the number made. The furthest from Paddington in these early days was Bridgwater, quite an important town in its own right and also convenient for the branch of the Somerset and Dorset Railway which ran across the Somerset Fens to Glastonbury and beyond.

In regard to coaches slipped from up trains, one notices, on the Birmingham main line, Hatton, a small station serving an unimportant village, from which a branch diverged to Stratford-upon-Avon. This was not only a tourist centre, but people were beginning to live there and work in Birmingham. At Warwick, too, trains were slipping coaches to work over the same branch line. However, the most noticeable slipping place was Reading, through which all GWR up expresses passed at this time, from north-west, west or south-west. It was a convenient place for changing trains for passengers proceeding to any point on the main line between Twyford and Ealing. It was a junction, too, where many other important routes met - westwards up the Kennet valley through Newbury to Hungerford and Devizes (a route later to become part of a main line

(Circular No. 382.)

GREAT WESTERN RAILWAY.

REGULATIONS AS TO THE WORKING SLIP COACHES.

1. The Guard in charge of a Slip Coach will be held responsible for seeing, before starting, that the Slip connection is in good working order, and free from grit or dirt, and also that it is properly fixed for slipping; he must satisfy himself before starting from the last Station before the Coach is slipped that the proper Tail Disc or Lamp is attached in the rear of the Coach or Coaches he is appointed to work. During the Journey he must always keep a sharp look-out so as to be prepared to act instantly in case of need.

2. **Immediately after slipping the Coach, the Guard must apply his break as hard as he can,** in order to let the Train get well ahead of the Slip Coach, so that in the event of the Train being unexpectedly stopped, he may have a sufficient distance to stop in, without running into the Train. The Carriage should never be allowed to run into the Carriage run slowly into the Station. Between sunset and daylight the Guard must exhibit a White Light from the Front Window of the Slip Coach, until the Coach stops at the Station.

3. In the event of the Slip Connection becoming disconnected on the Journey, the Guard must immediately apply his break to get the Slip Coach clear of the Train, as before stated, and unless he is within such a distance of a Station ahead that the Slip Coach will run into it, he must stop as soon as possible and go back immediately to the Station in the rear for assistance, taking his Detonators and Hand Signals with him to stop any coming Train. He should leave the Coach as soon as he can get down with safety, so as to get back with as little delay as possible to stop any coming Train. He must, however, take care to fasten his break down as tight as possible before he leaves the Coach. In the event of there being a Station ahead within such a distance that the Slip Coach will run up to it, it must be allowed to do so.

4. If from any cause the Guard finds he cannot Slip the Coach at the proper place, he must immediately give a Signal to the Head Guard to stop the Train, by using a red flag by day, or a red lamp by night. The Head Guard of the Train must always look back on the off side of his Train, at the proper place for the Coach to be Slipped, to see that it is properly detached, but he must not make any attempt to stop the Train unless he gets a Signal from the Guard of the Slip Coach to do so. **After the Guard of the Slip Coach has once given a Signal to the Head Guard to stop the Train he must not make any further attempt to detach the Coach until the Train has stopped.**

5. If from any cause he cannot get the Head Guard's attention in sufficient time to stop the Train at the Station, he must not make any further attempt either to stop the Train or Slip the Coach, but allow it to be carried through.

6. Should the Guard observe any defect in the Slip Coach connections, or from any cause he is prevented from implicitly complying with these instructions, he must immediately report full particulars to his Superintendent, and also on his journal.

7. In order to prevent Passengers being conveyed to the wrong Station, Guards working Slip Coaches must examine all Tickets before the Train is started.

DISTINCTIVE TAIL SIGNALS TO BE ATTACHED TO SLIP COACHES.

8. In order to enable the Switchmen at the Block Stations to see more readily whether a Slip Coach has broken away or not, all Slip Coaches in future will carry, instead of the usual Tail Lamps, **a Double Disc by day, and two Tail Lamps by night,** one above the other, to distinguish them from the Double Red Light (one beside the other) carried by a Train preceding a Special.

DAY SIGNAL.   NIGHT SIGNAL.

9. When the Coach for two different Stations are **attached to one Train, the first Coach,** or that going to the more distant Station, will carry a **Double Red Disc by day, and a Double Red Lamp by night,** as shown above, and the second Coach, or that to be slipped first, will carry **a Green and Red Disc by day, and a Green and Red Lamp by night,** thus:—

DAY SIGNAL.   NIGHT SIGNAL.

10. When from accident, a **Slip Coach becomes detached from a Train,** the Signalman in the first Signal-box which the Train passes without the Slip Coach, must signal to the next Signal-box ahead to stop the Train, when if the Train is all right, the Signalman at that box will Telegraph on to the next box, "**Slip Coach broken away, Train gone on without it,**" which message must be repeated from box to box, as far as the Slip Coach would have run, and the Train must be signalled and the Line cleared in the usual way, and if the Slip Coach has to be sent on by Special Engine it must be signalled as if it were another or Special Train.

11. Slip Coaches must be sent with the Trains by which they are arranged to run, whether there are any passengers for the Station at which they have to be slipped or not, but should it arise that from any cause a Slip Coach, which is running regularly, is not to be slipped, but the Train is to be stopped instead, the same Signals as the Slip Coach itself would have carried must be put on the last vehicle of the Train for the distance over which the Slip Coach would have run, and these Signals must be taken off at the Station where the Coach would have been slipped, and the ordinary Tail Lamp must then be attached.

12. The Special Discs or Lamps received at any Station on a Slip Coach must in every case be returned with the Coach, and any irregularity in working them must be immediately reported.

13. When it is necessary to arrange for a Coach to be slipped at a Station where Coaches are not usually slipped, an advice must be previously issued to all Stations and Block Cabins between the last stopping and the Station where the Coach may have to be slipped, by the Divisional Superintendent. The Station Masters, on receipt of such advice, must immediately advise the permanent way gangers.

14. When a Train, marked in the Working Time Book to convey Slip Coaches, is running late, and an extra Train has to be despatched in advance of it, from any intermediate Station, the first part must be considered the special, and will carry the "Special" Lamp in front, and the "Double Red" at the rear of the Train, to denote that the Ordinary Train is to follow, and will stop at the same Stations where Coaches are usually slipped. The **second** or late portion of the Train to convey the Slip Coaches (furnished with the Slip Coach Discs), to be slipped at the proper places in the usual way.

15. The Superintendents must satisfy themselves (1) that all Guards appointed to work Slip Coaches are well acquainted with the duty and the places where they have to Slip Coaches; and that a copy of these instructions is handed to each Guard; (2) that the Switchmen in their respective divisions are supplied with a copy of this notice, and that they understand what Tail Signals will be carried by Trains to which Slip Carriages are attached. Each man's receipt to be taken for the copy of notice.

G. N. TYRRELL,
Superintendent of the Line.

Circulars Nos. 245 and 344 are hereby cancelled.

shortening the journey to Devon and Cornwall), south-westward to Basingstoke where one linked with trains to Salisbury, Southampton and Bournemouth, and the South Eastern and Chatham's long branch from Redhill, through Dorking and Guildford to Reading, which gave access from GWR territory to the towns of West Surrey, Sussex and Kent and the long holiday coast from Margate to Portsmouth, as well as the short sea crossing to the Continent. Not surprisingly the daily slips at Reading eventually reached two figures and remained there until World War I.

Of all the GWR slip services, one of the longest-enduring was that at Wantage Road, between Didcot and Swindon. This was the nearest station to the market town of Wantage in Berkshire which, though on a main road between Oxford and Hungerford, was not so handily placed for a journey to or from the Metropolis. A number of trains stopped there in both directions, but they were slow; however, the 9.00 am from Paddington to the west carried a coach at its rear which was slipped there about an hour and a half later, providing the most convenient service of the day. One can credibly imagine what happened at 10.30 each weekday morning. Private carriages, cabs and an omnibus* would be clustered in the forecourt, the horses snorting and occasionally stamping their feet. Soon the 9.00 am from Paddington would be heard in the distance, non-stop between Didcot and Swindon, alerting coachmen, drivers and station porters to the fact that the slip portion was also on its way. Eventually the latter would glide into the platform and draw to a halt. Porters would hurry towards it to see who might want help with baggage (for Victorians never travelled light) and the doors of the slip carriage would open. Top-hatted gentlemen, crinolined ladies and over-dressed children would emerge (the boys perhaps curious to know how they could have got there without an engine) and be shepherded down the platform towards the ticket barrier and exit, to be collected in the appropriate vehicles and taken southwards for two miles to Wantage, famous birthplace of Alfred the Great and equally famous home of the legendary Town Clerk, the limerick about whom it is scarcely necessary to quote here.

One may also note that the GWR was the first company to slip a coach on a cross-country line, the GW and L&NW Joint Line between Crewe and Newport via Shrewsbury, Hereford and Pontypool Road. At Church Stretton, for a while from 1868, sometimes one, sometimes two slips were made. No doubt the coach was taken on to Craven Arms Junction, where connections could be made with the lines to Bishops Castle, Much Wenlock and Central Wales, the latter reaching as far as Swansea. This service, however, was discontinued in 1895.

The London and North Western Railway (LNWR) was slow in adopting slipping, beginning with detachments first at Watford, then at Blisworth for Northampton, then later at Leighton Buzzard. One of its slips, though not performed with daily regularity but occasionally as required, deserves mention, since it not only lasted over many years but was also unique. It offered a non-stop journey in the early afternoon from Euston to Leighton Buzzard for gentlemen who wished to join the hunt during the season. No doubt the Master of Fox Hounds would write to request its provision when he was apprised that there would be a sufficient number of clients from business houses and Board

---

* For many years from 1875 a steam tram was used for this purpose; it made a special journey from the town to meet the slip portion.

Great Western Railway.

Circular No. 426.

TAIL LAMPS GOING OUT ON SLIP COACHES.

Should a Train that has a Slip Coach on pass the Station in the rear of the Station at which the Coach is to be slipped, only showing one Tail Lamp on the last Coach, instead of two, the Signalman **must not** send on to the Station at which the Coach is to be slipped, the Signal "*Stop and examine Train,*" but must keep the block on and send the Signal "*Train passed without Tail Lamp*" to the Station in the rear, and will then ask on the Single Needle Instrument the Station at which the Coach should be slipped, "Has Slip Coach arrived?" If the reply is that the Slip Coach has arrived, he will immediately clear the Line to the Station in the rear, but if the answer is "**no**," he must immediately telegraph to the Station in the rear "Slip coach has broken away between this Station and yours."

Should a Train pass shewing no Tail Lamp at all, the Signal "*Stop and examine Train*" must be sent to the Station at which the Coach should be slipped in the usual manner.

G. N. TYRRELL,
Superintendent of Line.

PADDINGTON,
    19th November, 1880.

GREAT WESTERN RAILWAY.

(For the use of the Company's Servants only.)

WORKING OF SLIP COACHES

BETWEEN

LONDON and the undermentioned STATIONS.

WINTER 1885,

And until further notice.

NARROW GAUGE.

Train.	From	Attached at Station.	Attached at Time.	Coaches Slipped at Station.	Coaches Slipped at Time.	HOW THEY WORK AFTER BEING SLIPPED.	No. of Slips required.
4.45 p.m.	London	Paddington ..	4.45 p.m.	Leamington ..	6.58 p.m.	Forms Knowle Slip on 6.30 p.m. ex Paddington ..	
6.30 p.m.	London	Leamington ..	9.15 p.m.	Knowle ..	9.33 p.m.	Knowle dep 9.45 p.m.; Birmingham arr. 10.15 p.m	
7. 5 a.m.	Wolverhampton	Birmingham ..	7.30 a.m.	Warwick.. ..	7.56 a.m.	Warwick dep. 9.25 a.m.; Leamington arr. 9.30 a.m.	
12.15 p.m.	Chester	Leamington ..	3. 7 p.m.	Reading	4.42 p.m.	Forms Maidenhead Slip for 4.25 p.m. from Chester	2 Slips.
4.25 p.m.	Chester	Reading	9.50 p.m.	Maidenhead ..	10. 8 p.m.	Maidenhead dep. 10.25 p.m.; Windsor arr. 10.55 p.m., Windsor dep. 7 50 a.m. next day; Paddington arr. 8.52 a.m.	
4.25 p.m.	Chester	Birmingham ..	7.25 p.m.	Warwick.. ..	7.53 p.m.	Warwick dep. 8.58 p.m.: Leamington arr. 9.3 p.m., dep. 9.45 p.m.; Birmingham arr. 10.45 p.m. ..	1 Slip.
7.10 a.m.	Chester	Birmingham ..	10. 5 a.m.	Hatton	10.30 a.m.	Hatton dep. 10.38 a.m.; Stratford arr. 11.5 a.m. dep 11.40 a.m.; Hatton arr. 12.5 p.m., dep 12.9 p.m.; Birmingham arr. 12.55 p.m...	
1.30 p.m.	Chester	Birmingham ..	3.55 p.m.	Hatton	4.18 p.m.	Hatton dep. 4.27 p.m.; Stratford arr. 4.49 p.m., dep. 5.10 p.m.; Hatton dep. 5.40 p.m., Birmingham arr. 6.30 p.m. ..	2 Slips.
4.25 p.m.	Chester	Birmingham ..	7.25 p.m.	Banbury	8.28 p.m.	Banbury dep. 9.22 a.m. next day; Birmingham arr. 10.33 a.m...	
5. 5 p.m.	Birmingham ..	Birmingham ..	5. 5 p.m.	Hatton	5.38 p.m.	Hatton dep. 5.40 p.m.; Stratford arr. 6.5 p.m., dep. 6.15 p.m.; Hatton arr. 6.40 p.m., dep. 7.25 p.m.; Birmingham arr. 8.15 p.m.	1 Slip.
7. 5 a.m.	Wolverhampton	Oxford	9. 5 a.m.	Reading	9.40 a.m.	Reading dep. 1.30 p.m. See 10.0 ex Bristol .. .	
9.35 a.m.	Bristol	Swindon	10.50 a.m.	Reading	11.42 a.m.	Reading dep. 11.48 a.m.; Swindon arr. 1.0 p.m.	1 Slip.
10. 0 a.m.	Bristol	Reading	1.30 p.m.	Slough	1.55 p.m.	Windsor arr. 2.8 p.m., dep. 3.35 p.m.; Paddington arr. 4.36 p.m., ditto dep. 7.10; Didcot dep. 10.45 p.m.; Oxford arr. 11.10. p.m.	1 Slip.
1.45 p.m.	London	Paddington ..	1.45 p.m.	Slough	2.20 p.m.	Windsor arr. 2.30 p.m., dep. 4.10 p.m.; Paddington arr. 4.55 p.m. ..	1 Slip.
5.10 p.m.	London	Paddington ..	5.10 p.m.	Taplow	5.43 p.m.	From Taplow to Maidenhead at 5.55 p.m.; depart next day 9.20 a.m.; Paddington arr. 10.35 a.m.	1 Slip.
5.10 p.m.	London	Paddington ..	5.10 p.m.	Slough	5.35 p.m.	Slough dep. 5.38 p.m.; Windsor arr. 5.45 p.m., dep. 9.5 a.m. next day; Paddington arr. 9.40 a.m.	1 Slip.
6.20 p.m.	London	Paddington ..	6.20 p.m.	Slough	6.48 p.m.	Windsor arr. 7.0 p.m.; dep. 9.5 a.m. next day; Paddington arr. 9.40 a.m. ..	1 Slip.
6.20 p.m.	London	Paddington ..	6.20 p.m.	Twyford	7. 4 p.m.	Henley arr. 7.22 p.m., dep. 10.10 a.m. next day; Paddington arr. 11.45 a.m.	1 Slip.
6.30 p.m.	London	Paddington ..	6.30 p.m.	Taplow	7. 5 p.m.	Taplow dep. 7.10 p.m.; High Wycombe arr. 7.44, dep. 8.35 p.m.; Paddington arr. 10.15 p.m. ..	1 Slip.
1.30 p.m.	Chester	Birmingham ..	3.55 p.m.	Fenny Compton	4.50 p.m.	On Saturdays only, back to Birmingham by 6.20 p.m. ex Oxford	1 Slip.
9. 0 a.m.	Chester	Birmingham ..	12. 5 p.m.	Knowle ..	12.20 p.m.	Third Wednesday in each month. Knowle dep. 1.35 p.m.; Birmingham arr. 2.5 p.m.	1 Slip.
2.15 p.m.	Shrewsbury ..	Shrewsbury ..	2.15 p.m.	Church Stretton	2.39 p.m.	Returns to Salop by 5.25 p.m. ex Hereford } Except	1 Slip.
5.55 p.m.	Shrewsbury ..	Shrewsbury ..	5.55 p.m.	Church Stretton	6.19 p.m.	Returns to Salop by 5.25 p.m. ex Hereford } on Fridays The coaches working down on Friday are returned by 7.30 a.m. ex Hereford, Saturdays.	
10. 0 a.m.	London	Paddington ..	10. 0 a.m	Slough	10.33 a.m.	Windsor arr. 10.42 a.m., dep. 1.0 p.m.; Paddington arr. 1.37 p.m.	1 Slip.

BROAD GAUGE.

Train.	From	Attached at Station.	Attached at Time.	Coaches Slipped at Station.	Coaches Slipped at Time.	HOW THEY WORK AFTER BEING SLIPPED.	No. of Slips required.
9. 0 a.m.	Paddington ..	Didcot	10.18 a.m.	Wantage Road	10.30 a.m.	Wantage Road dep. 2.38 a.m. by 4.5 p.m. Plymouth Goods; Didcot arr. 2.53 a.m.	1 Slip.
12. 9 p.m.	Bristol	Swindon	1.18 p.m.	Reading	2. 4 p.m.	Reading dep. 4.0 p.m.; Paddington arrive 5.5 p.m.; dep. for Swindon 5.0 p.m. next day; Swindon arr. 6.50 p.m. ..	1 Slip.
5.34 p.m.	Bristol	Swindon	2 ? p.m.	Didcot	7. 9 p.m.	Didcot dep. 9.10 a.m., per Goods train, next day Swindon arr. 10.5 a.m.	1 Slip.
3. 0 p.m.	London	Bristol	5.41 p.m.	Bridgwater ..	6.19 p.m.	Bridgwater dep. 11.49 a.m., Bristol arr. 1.5 p.m. the next day	1 Slip.

NOTE.—The greatest attention must be paid to the working of these Coaches, by the Station Masters, the Carriage and Wagon Department, and the Guards, and a Special Report must be made to the Superintendent of the Division in which each Coach should arrive, of any Slip Coach not coming by the appointed Train, and the Guard of the Train must also notice it specially on his Report. Spare Slip Coaches to be kept at Swindon, Oxford, Birmingham, Reading, or Paddington; and any Station receiving a Slip Coach out of course must send it to one of the nearest Stations, and Report to the Divisional Superintendent.

When it is necessary to use a "Slip Coach" as a Break in an Ordinary Train, at busy times, attention should be paid to the selection of the Train, in order to ensure the "Slip Coach" being returned and available for its proper use.

The numbers of Slip Coaches are as follows :—

BROAD GAUGE :—41, 48, 213, 241, 251, 255, 256, 257, 258, 263, 264, 480, 481, 482, and 483.

NARROW GAUGE :—48, 110, 111, 112, 113, 114, 115, 116, 117, 118, 119, 143, 208, 239, 246, 312, 313, 321, 322, 323, 324, 344, 361, 501, 502, 503. 504, 505, 506, 507, 508 and 509.

PADDINGTON, *November*, 1885.

G. N. TYRRELL, *Superintendent of the Line.*

R. D. 68-453 P.

JUDD & Co., Printers, Doctors' Commons, London.

rooms in London who wished to revive their jaded energies with a little excitement. One would like to have been present as these eminent persons boarded the first class compartments, pulled down the blinds, changed into hunting pink, raised the blinds again and then smoked their cigars as their coach hurried through the Middlesex and Hertford countryside behind a 'Jumbo' or a Webb compound, exchanging opinions about politics and high society until the moment of slipping. At Leighton Buzzard no doubt grooms awaited them on the platform, and their mounts in the courtyard, and away they would go to the meet; financial killings would then be followed by a vulpine one somewhere in the recesses of South Bedfordshire.

The LNWR's associate, the Lancashire & Yorkshire Railway (L&YR), also adopted slipping slowly; from a single one in 1886 the number rose gradually to eight in 1900. Most were from westbound trains at Rochdale, where portions were detached to take the slow road by way of Bolton to Liverpool, stopping at several stations on the way, while the main part of the train went on to Manchester and then ran fast to Liverpool. The L&YR was unusual in announcing in its timetables not only the fact of a slip being made, but also the number of vehicles to be slipped. Though it never became a prolific user of slip coaches, the L&YR was unusually persistent; alone among the companies which later united to form the London, Midland and Scottish system it reintroduced slipping at the end of World War I, and these slips were continued after the company itself had ceased to exist as a separate entity.

The Midland Railway's (MR) adoption of slipping began with what looks to have been an outburst of enthusiasm. In 1885 it had none at all; the following year saw a single one at St Albans; in 1888 the number peaked to an astonishing 25. There was a subsequent lessening to as few as five in 1900; subsequently it was to rise again. Most slips were from up trains. In the peak year the MR slipped carriages at more places than any other railway was then doing - 18 as compared with the GWR's 16. A list of them shows that quite a few were on the cross-country main line from Derby to Bristol. The complete list includes Ambergate, Ashchurch, Berkeley Road, Blackwell, Bromsgrove, Cudworth, Defford, Harpenden, Heeley, Kettering, Luton, Market Harborough, Melton Mowbray, Oakham, Rotherham, St Albans, Syston and Wigston. Other slips in other years were made at Chesterfield, Leicester, Loughborough, Saxby, Sharnbrook, Stonehouse and Tamworth. The sudden explosion of 1888 must clearly have been the consequence of a policy decision, the later tailing-off indicating second thoughts. One wonders where all the needed slip carriages came from - whether they were specially built or whether existing brake composite coaches were suitably modified.

On the Great Northern Railway (GNR) slipping seems to have begun as early as 1864* and built up considerably until the end of the 1880s. According to Acworth's *Railways of England* (1889) the GNR in this year slipped more coaches daily than any other railway; the 5.30 pm from Kings Cross was noteworthy in that it 'slips a carriage for Huntingdon off a portion which is itself slipped at Peterborough, while at Grantham it attaches a fresh slip, only in its turn to drop it off at Newark; then at Retford it picks up another, which is left at Worksop.' GNR slipping subsequently began to lessen until, early in the following

---

* In the earlier timetables the word 'slip' was not used; instead appeared the statement: 'Passengers for _ _ _ _ _ _ must get into the last carriage at _ _ _ _ _ _.'

century, it had dwindled to one a day. Unlike the MR the GNR slipped mainly at principal stations, Potter's Bar and Essendine being exceptions.

Hitchin, the junction for the Cambridge branch, had as many as eight slips in 1880; one of these, off the 5.05 pm from King's Cross to Peterborough, became so well-filled that it had to be replaced by a separate train. Hatfield had as many as six in 1882. One curious feature of the GNR service in 1887 was the possibility of making the shortest journey in a slip carriage ever to be timetabled in Great Britain. One could board a train at New Barnet at 5.24 pm and be slipped at Potter's Bar, only 3½ miles further on, a few minutes later. Further down the line Essendine became for a while a place of frequent slipping, since here connections could be made for Stamford, a few miles along a branch to the south-west, and Bourne, some distance to the east on the Midland and Great Northern Joint Line to King's Lynn and Norwich. Right through this period Essendine enjoyed at least two slip services daily, rising to six between 1877 and 1885. 1883 was the GNR's peak year for slipping, when 30 slips were made at 12 stations.

The Great Eastern Railway (GER) also embraced the practice of slipping, but unlike the GNR and MR it did so gradually, reaching its zenith early the following century. The first slip service was at Chelmsford in 1872; the number then rose and gradually fell again to one in 1900. The second station to be so favoured was Tottenham, beginning in 1877; in all cases these were from up trains, the detached portion going on to St Pancras. In 1885 there were four such slips and the number rose to six in 1896. At Broxbourne the number of detachments, from down and up trains, varied from 1887 to 1900 between two and three, following a long period when they had been made only on Saturdays; all were for the benefit of the Hertford branch. From 1887, too, Harlow received slip portions on Mondays, Wednesdays and Saturdays during the winter months - a pattern which endured almost until World War I. Bishop's Stortford had a slip service from 1876 until the end of the century - in some years, two - serving the branch to Dunmow. At Audley End a slip for the Saffron Walden branch began in 1877, and a second one was added in 1883.

On the main line to Norwich, as well as the Chelmsford slips already mentioned, there were others in other years. Witham had one briefly, on Wednesdays only, serving the branch to Braintree, during 1875-1876; then, after a long interval, one was again established there from the evening express to Norwich. Mark's Tey, the station for the Sudbury and Bury St Edmunds branch, had a single one daily from 1875, increasing to two in 1891 and three in 1897. Colchester, the changing point for the Clacton branch, was served by one from a London-Harwich boat train in 1878, which continued for 32 years; a year and a half later there were three, and in 1884 four after which the number varied, peaking at six in 1897. Manningtree, for Harwich, was also briefly a slipping point during 1877-1878, after which the slip was transferred to Colchester, the former station being a very awkward place for this kind of operation since the main train, itself proceeding to Harwich (the slip being for Ipswich) had to slow to 10 mph for the sharp curve. Bentley also had a short-lived slip service during 1876-1877 for the Hadleigh branch.

One curious slip on GER metals took place for some years - it is not clear when it began or finished - which did not appear in the public timetable since it did not happen at a station; the mid-day train from Peterborough to Ely slipped a portion for Norwich at Ely North Junction. It is not clear what advantage this might have had over a detachment in Ely station once the train had stopped there, for the latter is only 1½ miles beyond the junction. Evidently it was eventually considered unnecessary, for after 1894 the detachment was made at Ely.

The North Eastern Railway took to slipping with no great enthusiasm, doing so in only three places. A morning westbound express from Hull to Normanton slipped a portion at Selby between 1871 and 1877. From the latter year until the end of the century one was slipped at Tweedmouth for the branch to Kelso. (One wonders whether it was the same vehicle from the discontinued Selby slip.) There also appears to have been one at Warkworth, though it was not described as such in the timetable, over some 20 years during the 1870s, 1880s and 1890s, from an evening semi-fast from Newcastle to Berwick; presumably it went on to Alnwick.

The Manchester, Sheffield and Lincolnshire Railway (MS&L) began to slip carriages in 1886 and continued to the end of the century, though never in large numbers. At this time the GNR was running through trains to Manchester by way of Retford, where they passed on to the MS&L route, and from these there were slips in both directions at Worksop between 1886 and 1899. From 1893 to 1899 there were also slips at various times at Penistone, the junction for Huddersfield, and Godley Junction, just short of London Road, Manchester, for Manchester Central. In 1899 the MS&L, having completed its new extension to London, blossomed out as the Great Central Railway, which was to continue to slip coaches, though not to the extent of its predecessor.

The North British Railway was the first Scottish line to slip carriages and also the first to discontinue doing so. Most slips were made on the Waverley route between Edinburgh and Carlisle - at Gorebridge, 12 miles south of Edinburgh near Falahill summit, at Stow, six miles short of Galashiels, and at Longtown, north of Carlisle, at various times between 1870 and 1893. There was also one at Drem from an eastbound train from Edinburgh, for North Berwick, from 1876 to 1893, and one at Polmont from 1873 to 1876 from an Edinburgh-Glasgow train. In the case of the Waverley route, the need to keep loadings light over a very heavily-graded route may have had something to do with their cessation.

The Glasgow and South Western Railway, so far as slipping was concerned, did little more than put its toes in the water. From June 1898 to September 1901 the evening express from Glasgow (St Enoch) to Stranraer, non-stop between Paisley and Prestwick, slipped a coach at Irvine, which continued to Ayr, stopping at all stations.

South of the Thames the London and South Western Railway (LSWR) made use of slip coaches to a small extent, mostly on suburban services and with evening departures from Waterloo. There had briefly been one for the Chertsey branch, during the 1860s, and this, with another, was re-introduced between 1887 and 1902, either Weybridge or Walton-on-Thames being the point of slipping. From 1891 to 1902 the 5.40 pm from Waterloo to Reading via Staines slipped a portion at Feltham for Ashford (Middlesex). Further afield, from 1894 a morning train from Waterloo to Portsmouth detached a carriage at Petersfield, while between 1896 and 1900 there was a daily slip at Winchester from the 4.55 pm from Waterloo to Bournemouth. However, after 1902 the LSWR lost interest in slipping and never resumed the practice.

The South Eastern Railway made a moderate use of slipping - indeed, in its earliest days, when it had been one of the pioneers of the practice, a very considerable use, amounting between 1863 and 1865 to 11 slips daily, most of which were at Caterham Junction to serve the Caterham branch - with a gradual diminution, however, between 1875 and 1898 (when the company made a working union with the Chatham line) from four to one, the latter being at Ashford from the evening boat express, both on weekdays and Sundays. Earlier, the two morning boat trains had also slipped portions there. Sevenoaks had a slip service during 1871-1880 - in some years two. Tonbridge had between one and three between 1861 and 1867, and occasionally one on Sundays as well. Paddock Wood in some years received slips from both down and up trains for the Maidstone branch. One notes that there were Sunday slips at as many as three places; other lines were in general more Sabbatarian.

The London, Chatham and Dover Railway (LC&DR) never had more than five slips daily; more usually there were three or four, Beckenham Junction, Chatham and Faversham receiving them in the down direction and Herne Hill in the up, the slipped portion then proceeding to whichever of the LC&DR's main London termini the main train was not bound for. The Herne Hill slips were the nearest to a London terminus made anywhere in Britain, apart from the short-lived slip on the GWR at Westbourne Bridge mentioned earlier.

The London, Brighton and South Coast Railway, though it had pioneered slipping in 1858, showed some caution in extending the practice, but over the years made more and more use of it, the daily number increasing from three in 1875 to nine in 1900. The LB&SCR was in fact the only British company in which the increase was unbroken right up to the outbreak of World War I. At one time or another during 1858-1900 seven stations were served. Like the SER and LC&DR this line had both a City and a West End terminus, and some up trains slipped at East Croydon or Sutton for whichever of them the main train was not going to.* The chief slipping place was Haywards Heath, just south of which the Eastbourne and Hastings line diverges to the east, along which the detached portions mostly ran.

All the above slip services were on important main line railways which ran express trains. Rather surprisingly, one less important line which could boast no really fast trains, the Furness Railway, not merely adopted slipping but persisted in the practice until 1916. Most of its slips were at Grange-over-Sands, beginning with two in either direction in 1887 but gradually diminishing to two in summer and one in winter. There was also a slip at Ulverston, in the summer only, from 1888 onwards, that connected with a steamer service to the Isle of Man - perhaps the only slip carriage service ever instituted which was specifically for steamer passengers. From 1891 to 1899 a coach was slipped at Askam from a Barrow-Whitehaven train, which followed the latter, stopping at all stations to Millom. Arnside also had one in 1890 and Dalton in 1891, both

---

* In the April 1957 issue of the *Railway Magazine* M.D. Greville recalled that 'as a boy I always got a certain thrill seeing at East Croydon the slipping of the Victoria sections of the 8.45 am from Brighton and the 8.30 from Eastbourne. Those slips were very impressive; they were not single coaches but considerable portions of those trains.'

during the summer.

There does not seem to have been much allusion to slipping in railway literature during these days. I cannot forbear from quoting the only one I have been able to find, from one of E.L. Ahrons' *Railway Magazine* articles, which were later gathered into six books entitled *Locomotive and Train Working in the Nineteenth Century*. In dealing with the Great Western in broad-gauge days, he remarks:

> On the London turn they [the broad gauge engines of the 2-4-0 '2201' class] came down with the 5.10 pm express from Paddington to Reading, a train that probably conveyed more slip coaches than anything in that way hitherto invented. Slip coaches were always a feature with the Great Western Railway, and the 5.10 pm enabled the authorities to carry out unlimited ideas in this direction. We left Paddington with 16 six-wheeled coaches, with a 45-minute non-stop schedule to Reading, 36 miles. At Slough we slipped five coaches for Windsor, dropped three more at Taplow (where these went to I do not know), shed another three at Twyford for Henley, and finally pulled up triumphantly in Reading station with only five of our original 16 carriages. But the fun did not end at this point, for we generally managed to arrive with a number of passengers who ought to have been in the Slough, Taplow or Twyford slips, and the noisy objurgations which these people emitted when they discovered that they had arrived at where they did not want to be can be better imagined than described. Despite the most frantic efforts on the part of a perspiring army of Paddington ticket collectors, some five per cent of the passengers either got rounded up into or stowed themselves away in the wrong portions.*

Ahrons' penchant for humour, of his own somewhat pawky variety, probably got the better of a desire for strict accuracy, but no doubt he was exaggerating something that often happened. The days when carriages were clearly labelled with large destination boards had not yet arrived, nor were there as yet any public address systems.

A GWR multi-portion form, dating from the last century, issued to the crew of a train conveying a slip coach and used when the train could not slip because of foggy conditions. Portion 1 was retained by the issuer, the station master at the starting point of the train. The note on the slip guard's portion indicates that the coupling was to be placed over the hook at the rear of the train, not over the slip coach hook.

---

* Ahrons: Op. cit.: Vol IV: pp.55-56.

Chapter Three

Towards the Zenith of Slipping:
1901-1914

The Edwardian period, and the four years that followed it before World War I broke out, were in many respects a climax in regard to railway travel. They saw the final extension of the British main line railway system, in the making of new lines to shorten existing express routes; they witnessed a rapid spread in dining and sleeping car provision; during them there was a general increase in the average speeds of services between the larger centres of population; electrification began on routes carrying a large number of commuters; long-distance holiday travel increased greatly in popularity. Not surprisingly the use of slip coach services also greatly increased. The Great Western had half as many again in 1914 as in 1900. On the London and North Western, which had none at all in 1895, there were 18 in 1914; on the Midland the figure rose from five to 21, on the London, Brighton & South Coast from nine to 27; on the Caledonian from none at all to 12. The Great Eastern peaked to a maximum of 26 in 1904, declined to 16 in 1910 and then began to rise again. Only on the Great Northern was there a definite 'bucking of the trend'; here the number fell from six to one. Given that the railway was the most convenient, fastest and most widely available means of long distance travel, it was no doubt inevitable that slip coach use should keep pace with general use. The forces that later arose to make for diminution and discontinuance were not yet in evidence.

Foremost among the slipping companies, as during the previous century, was the GWR, whose 49 slips daily in 1900 rose to 72 in 1914 after peaking at 79 in 1908. On this line two slip portions travelled further before being detached than happened on any other railway. In this regard one may refer to a readily-available source, *Bradshaw's Railway Guide* for April 1910, which is available in a slightly enlarged facsimile form. In this month there were 69 weekday slips, one on Saturdays only and one on Sundays only. 22 were made at distances over 100 miles from their starting point, eight at over 15 miles, while one, slipped at Carmarthen for Aberystwyth, almost achieved 200 miles attached to its parent train. This had had a forerunner in 1906, as a slip from the same train at the same place for Tenby.

Four and a quarter years later, on the eve of the War, the pattern had altered a little, since the new and shorter route to Birmingham had now been opened, from Old Oak Common Junction to Aynho Junction, and the trains from Paddington to the West Midlands and Birkenhead now followed it. At two stations along the cut-off route slips were made, at Princes Risborough and Bicester, but no up trains on this service slipped at Reading any more and the former slip at Oxford also disappeared. The slips at Hatton for Stratford-upon-Avon were halved in number, the latter town now having a much better direct service on the line from Birmingham through Henley-in-Arden. Slips from the London direction, on the other hand, made principally to give connections with Shakespeare's birthplace, increased from three to five. Otherwise the pattern was much the same as in 1910.

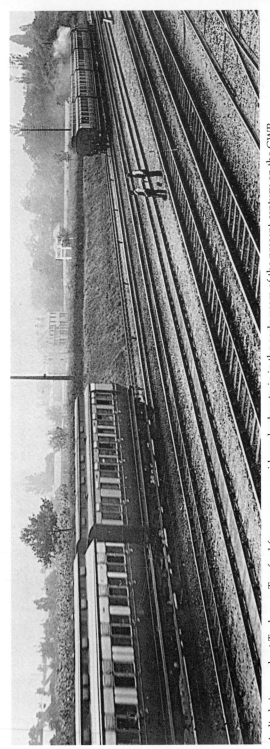

A slip being made at Taplow or Twyford from a non-corridor suburban train in the early years of the present century on the GWR.

GWR Museum, Swindon

Some of the GWR slips at this time call for particular mention. The detachments from down trains made at Westbury offered an alternative route to Weymouth to the shorter London and South Western one by way of Bournemouth, and some trains ran through from Paddington, but the fastest, quicker than any by the LSWR route except the 4.10 pm from Waterloo, was provided by the portion slipped from the 'Cornish Riviera Express', and one may imagine that many Londoners preferred to use it, especially if Paddington was nearer; the travelling comfort, in a slip carriage with a side corridor, was at least equal to that on the other line, the only deprivation was the lack of access to a restaurant car.* One of the slips at Newbury ran through to Southampton by way of the Didcot, Newbury and Southampton line; not many people would have chosen to make the whole journey by this route rather than from Waterloo, but for passengers from stations between Paddington and Reading, at which latter station the train stopped, it might very well have been convenient. The small station at Savernake had three slips, reflecting the fact that here the Midland and South Western Junction Line from Cheltenham to Andover crossed the GWR and that there was a station on it within easy reach of that of the larger company. The slip at Patney gave access to the interesting old Wiltshire town of Devizes, noted for its splendid archaeological museum, though perhaps better known as the residence of the young man with unequally-sized ears, celebrated in the famous limerick.

The slip from the morning Bristol express at Bath had the distinction at this time of providing the fastest slip carriage service in the country, at 59.3 mph; after the War it was to become even quicker. That at Kingham actually offered the fastest down service of the day between Paddington and Cheltenham, travelling over the north Cotswold line instead of the more circuitous route by way of Swindon and Gloucester. One of the four Taunton slips, from the 11.50 am from Paddington, was for a while during this period almost a train in itself, having four vehicles, one of which was a restaurant car, bound for Ilfracombe.

The slip at Pylle Hill needs special mention. It was made on the loop line that avoided Bristol (Temple Meads) station, and was not made from a passenger train but for the convenience of the Post Office, which ran an express mail service from Plymouth (where the mails from America were collected from a liner which touched there). Slipping a specially designed sorting carriage at Pylle Hill saved many minutes on the journey to London. The slipped vehicle, attached to another train, then proceeded towards the West Midlands. (See Appendix Seven for further remarks about this service.)

One turns now to the London and North Western Railway. Though on this line regularly-made slip services had disappeared by 1895, they had begun again the following year with a short-lived detachment at Cheddington, with another the year after that at Leighton Buzzard. Subsequently the build-up was comparatively rapid, reaching a total of 18 daily in 1910 and 19 in 1914. Apart from those at Rugeley and (for 2½ years only) Stafford, all were within 100 miles of London. The adjacent table gives the patterns of 1910 and 1914.

---

* The history of the slips made from the 'Cornish Riviera Express' during the period when they operated is discussed in Appendix Two.

The rear end of one of Churchward's 'Toplight' single-ended slip coaches built in September 1908. The square hinged flap below and to one side of the central window conceals the warning hooter.

J.H. Russell Collection

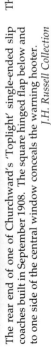

The rear end of one of Churchward's 'toplight' slip coaches.

GWR Museum, Swindon

Table One

Slip Detachments on the Great Western Railway:
April 1910 and July 1914

Place	1910	1914	Comments
Reading	10	10	All but one from up trains.
Hatton	6	3	Through to Stratford-upon-Avon, from up trains.
Slough	5	6	Through to Windsor. Plus 1 SO.
Banbury	5	6	All but one from down trains.
Taunton	4	4	
Bridgwater	4	3	Connection with S&DR line to Glastonbury.
Westbury	3	5	Includes one up slip & one made SuO.
Leamington Spa	3	5	
Chippenham	3	3	
Savernake	3	3	Connecting with trains on M&SWJR.
Wellington	3	3	
Twyford	2	3	Through to Henley-on-Thames.
Didcot	2	2	Connecting with trains to Oxford.
Newbury	2	2	One through to Southampton.
Warwick	2	1	Through to Stratford-upon-Avon.
Taplow	1	2	
Carmarthen	1	1	Through to Aberystwyth.
Bath	1	1	
Exeter	1	1	
Knowle	1	1	
Kingham	1	1	Through to Cheltenham.
Moreton-in-Marsh	1	1	
Maidenhead	1	1	For High Wycombe branch.
Tilehurst	1	2	Goes on to Cholsey & Moulsford.
Wantage Road	1	1	
Oxford	1	-	From up train from Birmingham.
Patney	1	-	Through to Devizes.
Princes Risborough	-	1	
Bicester	-	1	
Lapworth	-	1	
Pylle Hill, Bristol	1	1	From up Ocean Mail Post Office train, for Midlands.

Table Two

Slip Detachments on the London & North Western Railway:
April 1910 and July 1914

Place	1910	1914	Comments
Nuneaton	4	4	One up, three down, of which two went on to Buxton via Ashbourne.
Bletchley	4	3	All but one from up trains.
Blisworth	3	5	Including one from early newspaper train in 1914. Connections with Northampton.
Leighton Buzzard	2	2	Connections with Dunstable branch.
Rugby	3	-	Through to Leamington Spa.
Rugeley	1	1	Through to Shrewsbury & Welshpool.
Coventry	1	4	In 1914 two allowed restaurant car access to Slip coach passengers.

A slip coach from a down MR express decelerating as it runs into Loughborough on 26th July, 1911. A typical MR slip coach with clerestory, slip compartments at either end and no vestibules.

National Railway Museum

The slips at Nuneaton served Hinckley and Burton-upon-Trent and, by a somewhat meandering route, Uttoxeter, Ashbourne and Buxton Spa. The two portions which went through to the latter used the metals of two other lines to do so and provided a service more interesting than expeditious. The ones made at Bletchley connected with the cross-country line from Oxford to Cambridge; the one down slip went on to Banbury by a little-used branch line. The slips at Rugby for Leamington were competitive with the GWR service to that town in 1910, but after the latter had brought its short-cut route into operation they were no longer so, and were therefore withdrawn. The portion slipped at Rugeley from an afternoon express from Euston also strayed on to the lines of other companies on its continuation to Welshpool, first joining the LNW/GW route to beyond Shrewsbury; then, four miles from its destination, passing on to Cambrian Railway metals at Buttington Junction. The Coventry slips reflected the rapid growth in importance of this bicycle-manufacturing centre; not only did the number of them increase, but those travelling by the first morning and last evening services; were singularly fortunate, since early in 1914 the coach they travelled in became one with a vestibuled gangway connecting it with the parent train. Anyone wanting breakfast or dinner could therefore use the restaurant car and had time to enjoy a meal at leisure before returning, to the slip portion; the slip guard then sealed off the gangway connection from within his compartment before making the slip. This facility was to last for a few months only; then, with the advent of World War I, it was discontinued, and no resumption was made after 1918, nor did any other line adopt the practice, so far as is certainly known.

On the Midland Railway the two principal express routes, from St Pancras to the Midlands and North, and from Derby through Birmingham to Bristol, both had several stations served by slip portions; at one time or another during this period 17 enjoyed this facility, but the number had fallen to seven in April 1910, rising to ten in 1914. The adjacent table shows the position in the years 1903, 1910 and 1914.

Table Three
Slip Detachments on the Midland Railway:
July 1903, April 1910 and July 1914

Place	1903	1910	1914	Comments
Chesterfield	-	3	3	
Harpenden	1	-	-	
Kettering	5	-	2	
Loughborough	1	2	2	All from up trains.
Luton	1	2	3	All from up trains.
Melton Mowbray	1	2	2	All from down trains.
Oakham	*3	-	1	All from down trains.
Rotherham	1	2	1	(Station then known as Masborough.)
Saltaire	-	2	2	From up trains, going on to Bradford.
Saxby	1	-	-	Through to M&GN Joint Line.
Sharnbrook	1			Through to Wellingborough & Northampton.
St Albans	1	-	-	
Tamworth	-	2	2	
Wellingborough	-	-	1	Unusual in being slipped twice on a single southbound journey - see text.

* Plus one on Saturdays only.

A Great Eastern Railway slip from a down train near Broxbourne *c.* 1905. The slip portion of five coaches will proceed to Hertford. The locomotive is one of Holden's 2-4-0s rebuilt with a larger boiler and Belpaire firebox.   *Railway Magazine*

A GER slip being made, just as the train passes the distant signal before the target station *c.* 1905. Note the lamp within the disc indicating the rear of the slip portion.

Railway Magazine

The slip at Wellingborough in 1914 was unique, being slipped twice in the course of the same southbound journey. It was attached to an up express at Kettering, slipped seven miles further on at Wellingborough, re-attached there later to an up express from Manchester and slipped a second time at Luton after another 35 miles. Presumably passengers from the north were warned to 'change into the last coach' both at Kettering and Wellingborough.

It would appear that the MR, like the LNWR, contemplated the provision of slip coaches with vestibule connections, so that passengers in them could use a restaurant car; however, there is no evidence that any such vehicle actually came into use before the exigencies of World War I ended slipping altogether on this railway.*

On the North Eastern Railway slipping, infrequent before 1900, had during this period almost vanished. Only one was made, from a midday express from Newcastle, which slipped a carriage at about 2 pm at Tweedmouth for the Kelso branch, and even this was frequently omitted in summer, when a semi-fast train followed the express and stopped at Tweedmouth to connect with a train on the branch line. After 1905 this slip ceased entirely, leaving the NER with none at all.

The Great Northern, which had made so much use of slip coaches during the previous century, was now discarding the practice; while in 1901 there were six daily throughout the year, and another during the winter months at Doncaster, in 1902 there were four, in 1903 three, in 1904 two, and after 1905 only the Doncaster slip, off the up 'Flying Scotsman', remained.

On the Great Eastern Railway slip coach usage, though decreasing a little after peaking at a daily total of 25 in 1904, continued until 1914, falling and then tending to rise again before disappearing entirely in the last year of World War I. At one time or another 11 stations received slip portions. The table below shows the pattern in 1904, 1908, 1910 and 1914:

Table Four
Slip Detachments on the Great Eastern Railway:
1904, 1908, 1910 and 1914

Place	1904	1908	1910	1914	Comments
Audley End	2	2	2	2	Through to Saffron Walden.
Bishops Stortford	2	-	-	-	
Broxbourne	4	1	6	6	Through to Hertford.
Colchester	3	1	2	-	
Harlow	1	1	-	-	Winter service only.
Ingatestone	1	1	1	1	Saturdays excepted.
Mark's Tey	3	3	2	3	Ran through to or connected with Sudbury branch.
Shenfield	1	2	1	2	Ran through to Southend branch.
Tottenham	6	-	1	1	From up trains on Cambridge line, through to St Pancras
Waltham Cross	1	1	1	1	
Witham	1	-	1	1	

---

* See Appendix Eight for the pros and cons of this matter.

The front end of a GER slip coach; note the end windows, the two inner ones of which can be opened, and the draw-hook in the open position.   *Railway Magazine*

The slip coach for Nottingham, Lincoln and Cleethorpes, having just been detached from the 3.15 pm from Marylebone non-stop to Sheffield, draws into the platform at Leicester Central station. This coach was one of a pair built in 1911.   *Locomotive Publishing Co.*

The slips at Broxbourne, which increased to a considerable number, must have represented a considerable saving in engine use, for each was almost a train in itself, a 12-coach express going towards Cambridge slipping five vehicles for Ware and Hertford. Even longer slip portions were in theory permitted, but the actual maximum anywhere seems to have been five. They were, however, six-wheelers, weighing up to about 16 tons tare. Too heavy a slip portion, when braking was possible only on the front vehicle with the use of the hand brake (obligatory except in an emergency) would obviously have been inadvisable.

It was a Mark's Tey slip, of four six-wheelers, which was involved in one of the only two slip-carriage accidents on record. A full account of it appears in Chapter Eight.

The former Manchester, Sheffield and Lincolnshire Railway, which after the completion of the London extension to Marylebone had become the Great Central Railway, at first discontinued all its former slips except for one at Godley Junction, where the detached portion went on to Liverpool, and this lasted until June 1904. In July 1903 it began to slip a coach at Leicester from its 'flagship' train, the 3.25 pm from Marylebone, non-stop to Sheffield in under three hours. This carriage went on through Nottingham and Mansfield to the former Lancashire, Derbyshire and East Coast Railway and proceeded to Grimsby and Cleethorpes; however, in later years it terminated at Lincoln. Few people would have wished to travel it all the way from London to the Lincolnshire coast, the service from King's Cross being so much shorter and more convenient. The other important northbound GCR express, the evening train from London to Bradford, also for a short while in 1904 slipped a coach at Leicester. During 1903-1904 a southbound express non-stop from Sheffield to Marylebone slipped a coach at Nottingham which then went on to Leicester, stopping at all stations. From 1907 onwards the evening Bradford express slipped a coach at Woodford, which gave Stratford-upon-Avon a convenient through evening service, competitive with what the GWR could offer, and this lasted until World War I and was re-introduced after it. From July 1905 a through coach from Bournemouth was attached to the rear of a slip coach at Sheffield; both were then attached to the rear of the 3.15 pm (formerly 3.25 pm) express from Marylebone to Manchester and both were slipped at Penistone, to proceed to Huddersfield and Bradford; this service, too, lasted until the outbreak of the War. From October 1911 a northbound train from Nottingham also slipped a coach at Heath for Chesterfield. On Saturdays only, from October 1907 to June 1908, a commuter slip service was provided on the 1.40 pm from Marylebone, which was slipped at Amersham and went on to Great Missenden.

The Lancashire and Yorkshire Railway's slip services had peaked in 1889-1890 at eight, and remained at between six and eight until World War I. The following table shows the positions in four well-separated years:

Two coaches being slipped at Rochdale off the 9.40 am Bradford to Manchester and Liverpool on 19th October, 1913. The slip portion went on to Liverpool by way of Bolton, calling at all stations.

National Railway Museum

Table Five
Slip Detachments on the Lancashire and Yorkshire Railway
in 1904, 1908, 1910 and 1914

Place	1904	1908	1910	1914	Comments
Accrington	-	-	-	1	On three days each week, from the 4.25 pm Salford-Colne.
Blackburn	-	-	1	1	For Accrington, from a Blackpool-Colne train.
Kirkham	-	-	2	2	From Manchester-Blackpool expresses.
Midge Hall	1	1	1	1	From Liverpool-Preston train, for Blackburn.
Rochdale	7	5	2	2	From Leeds/Bradford trains to Manchester, to run all-stations to Liverpool.
Todmorden	-	-	1	1	

The L&YR was unusual in indicating the number of vehicles in each slip portion in its timetable: e.g. 'Passengers for Todmorden and Burnley direction travel in the rear three vehicles which will be slipped at Todmorden'. The slip from the 4.25 pm from Salford to Colne was probably the trickiest slip operation made at any time on any railway. The descent from Baxenden summit to Accrington was very steep - 1 in 40 right to the platform ends - and Accrington station itself was on a very sharp curve, so that the main train had to slow down almost to a crawl. Mr R.W. Rush, an expert on L&YR history, was kind enough to include the following remarks in a letter:

There used to be fun and games with the slip at Accrington off the 4.25 Salford-Colne express. Several times the slip didn't come off properly, and either stopped short of the platform or caught up the main train again - with the 10 mph speed limit through the station it was a very difficult operation. The station pilot engine (usually an 0-6-0 saddle tank) was always at hand at the junction in case anything went wrong. Three porters had to be stationed on No. 2 platform (the train went through platform 3) to pass a signal to the driver that the slip had come off, as, owing to the sharp curve, the driver could not see the rear of the train. Most of the other slip services took place on straight track; it was only at Accrington that there was any difficulty.

From 1910 right through the War years to 1919 the two evening business expresses from Manchester to the Fylde coast each slipped a portion at Kirkham, one going direct to Blackpool (Talbot Road station) while the main train went by the coast route via Lytham, four miles further, to Central station; the other went vice versa. In the case of the first, the slip portion actually arrived at Blackpool before the main train.

On the Furness Railway, where earlier there had been slips at as many as five places, during this period there were only two. At Grange-over-Sands there were two in summer and one in winter until 1909; after that, only one throughout the year. The Ulverston slip in connection with the boat service to the Isle of Man, mentioned in the previous chapter, also continued until 1905.

South of the Thames, the London continued its slips at Feltham* and Walton or Weybridge, mentioned also in the previous chapter, until 1902, and then ceased slipping altogether. The South Eastern and Chatham continued with a

---

* Though attached to the main train south of the Thames at Waterloo, the slip was actually made to the north of the river.

SE&CR third class brake carriage built at Ashford as a slip coach in 1908, with 'birdcage roof' above guard's compartment - characteristic of SE&CR practice. It is seen here some 40 years later being used as an ordinary brake third.   *D. Gould*

moderate number, as shown in the list below:

Table Six
Slip Detachments on the South Eastern and Chatham Railway
During 1905, 1908, 1910 and 1914

Place	1905	1908	1910	1914	Comments
Ashford	1	1	1*	1	For Hythe and Sandgate via Sandling Junction.
Farningham Road	-	-	1	-	For all stations to Chatham.
Faversham	1	1	1	2	
Herne Hill	2	2	2	1	
Shorncliffe	1	1	1	1	
Swanley	-	-	-	1	This replaced the earlier one at Farningham Road.

* Also made on Sundays.

The Herne Hill slips, from up commuter trains, like those made in the previous century, served whichever of the two main London termini the main train was not heading for. In addition to those listed above, from 1911 onwards there was also a slip from a down train on Fridays only at Paddock Wood, for the Maidstone branch.

Next to the GWR the London Brighton and South Coast Railway was the most consistent slip carriage user of all the pre-Grouping companies, and was to continue slipping at some stations right through to 1918. During the period under review the number trebled from nine to 27. The table below gives the pattern of increase as seen in five separate years:

Table Seven
Slip Detachments on the London, Brighton and South Coast Railway:
During 1905, 1908, 1910, 1912 and 1914

Place	1905	1908	1910	1912	1914	Comments
Arundel	-	-	-	-	1	
Ashurst	-	-	-	-	4	For Tunbridge Wells.
Barnham Junction	1	1	1	2	2	For Bognor.
East Croydon	2	-	2	2	2	From up trains, either for Victoria or London Bridge.
Haywards Heath	3	4	5	7	5	
Horley	1	1	2*	2*	2	For East Grinstead.
Polegate	-	4	4	6	6	From Eastbourne trains, for Hastings.
Preston Park	2	4	1	3	3	
Sutton	-	1	1	1	1	From an up train to Victoria, slipped for London Bridge.
Three Bridges	-	-	-	1	1	For Eastbourne.

* One was on Saturdays only.

A slip being made on the approach to Haywards Heath from a down train on the LB&SCR during the first decade of the 20th century.   *Author's Collection*

With as many as 27 slips made daily in 1914, the LB&SCR was second only to the GWR. It was among the most economy-conscious of the pre-War companies, and clearly saw slipping as a means of saving engine miles, of which in 1914 over 7,500 fewer were run weekly than would have been the case if an equal service had been supplied with no slips being made at all.

During these years, except right at the very end, the only Scottish company to engage in slipping was the Caledonian, which had had none at all at the turn of the century. Subsequently the pattern was as shown in the table below:

Table Eight
Slip Detachments on the Caledonian Railway
in 1904, 1908, 1910 and 1914

Place	1904	1908	1910	1914	Comments
Carluke	-	1	1	1	For commuters; went on to Lanark.
Cleghorn	-	-	-	1	For commuters; went on to Lanark.
Coupar Angus	-	2	2	1	For Blairgowrie.
Crieff Junction	-	2	2	2	For Crieff and Comrie. In 1914 it continued to St Fillan's.
Falkirk	-	1	1	1	From Edinburgh (Princes Street).
Guthrie	-	2	2	2	From Aberdeen, for stations to Arbroath.
Larbert	-	-	1	1	From Aberdeen-Glasgow express.
Lockerbie	2	-	3	3	Attached at Carlisle to trains from south of the Border.

The peak year was actually in 1911-1912, when there was also a down slip from a northbound express at Stirling. The Lockerbie slips are somewhat surprising, as although there was a branch thence to Dumfries the slipped portions did not make handy connections with it, and Lockerbie was a small place in itself, smaller then than now.

As hinted above, there is one other Scottish company to be mentioned, the Great North of Scotland Railway, on which until the summer of 1914 no slipping had ever taken place. Beginning on 1st June of that year, a carriage was slipped at Banchory from the 4.45 pm train from Aberdeen to Ballater. Elaborate instructions were sent to everyone concerned by the Passenger Superintendent, but the slip only lasted during the summer months, being discontinued in the autumn after the outbreak of War and never reinstated.

Finally, the Furness Railway continued to slip portions at Grange-over-Sands, two in summer and one in winter from down trains from Carnforth until 1910, after which there was only one, all the year round, from the 7.25 pm from Carnforth; this continued until 1916. The Cumbrian Railways' Association circular letter for February 1978 contains a personal reminiscence by George Taylor, who was a boy at the time, which is worth quoting:

> When meeting this train we used to wait with bated breath and listen for the clatter of the down home signal on its lattice post, while a quick glance westward confirmed that the down starter showed green. Soon there was a muted roar eastward, and belting past the signal box appeared the twin white headlamps of, probably, 6 foot 4-4-0 No. 37, which then swayed and roared through the station, leaving behind drifting smoke and steam and a diminuendo of sound westwards.

> Then, however, appeared another white lamp advancing almost silently through the thinning steam residue, and with a gentle hiss of brakes the slip came to a stand. 'All change!' yelled the porters on the platform - surely an unnecessary command - and the dozen or so Grange passengers got off. There followed an astounding performance after everyone had alighted, and one which I often lingered to see.

> The small amount of luggage and parcels were dumped from the guard's compartment, and the back-shunt banner signal moved to green (white was 'danger' on FR shunting signals). With two hefty porters with pinch bars, and a couple more pushing on the buffer beam, the slip coach was moved by muscle power into the goods yard, to be returned to Carnforth next day on the morning roadside good train. Knowing that Grange had a horse delivery dray, I have wondered why the horse did not round off his day's toil by deputising for the humans. I presume his driver had long packed up and gone home.

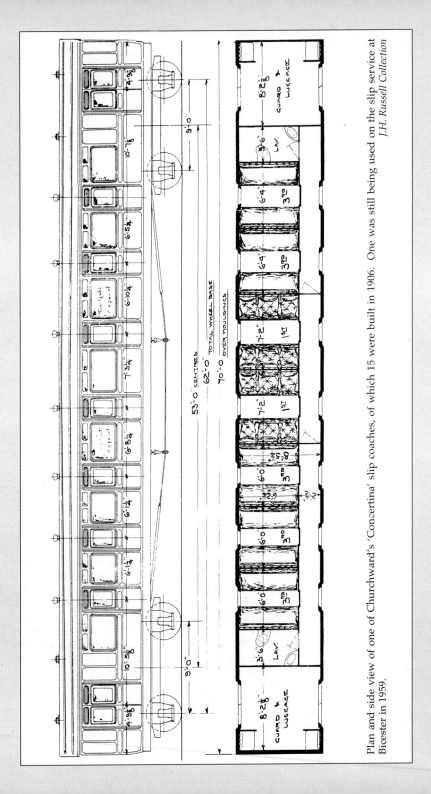

Plan and side view of one of Churchward's 'Concertina' slip coaches, of which 15 were built in 1906. One was still being used on the slip service at Bicester in 1959.

J.H. Russell Collection

Chapter Four

Slipping in Decline:
1914-1960

The table below shows how the practice of slipping carriages, which had built up to a maximum during the previous 55 years, first went into rapid decline during World War I, recovered again on some lines and then again declined during the inter-War years. It disappeared altogether during World War II, then came back to a certain extent on one line only, and finally vanished even from that.

Table Nine

Company	Number of weekday slips made during:						
	1916	1918	1922	1924	1928	1934	1938
GWR	34	-	31	47	40	22	20
LMSR[1]	27	5[2]	5[2]	6	-	-	-
LNER[3]	12	-	3	5	4	4	1
SR[4]	14	3	22	31	2	-	-

[1]. Includes the former LNWR, MR, L&YR, CR, G&SWR and HR.
[2]. All made on L&YR metals.
[3]. Includes the former GNR, NER, GER, GCR, NBR and GNSR.
[4]. Includes former LSWR, SE&CR and LB&SCR.

To interpret these figures: during World War I - slipping vanished by degrees from all lines except the L&YR and LB&SCR. On the former there was actually a daily increase from seven to nine before falling to five; on the latter there was a sharp drop from 27, first to 14, then to three. The enormous reduction over the four years of the War reflects the manpower problem which the companies faced. Slip coach usage had always been labour-intensive, and the consequence of railway employees enlisting in the armed forces, at first through volunteering and later through conscription, was that increasingly fewer men remained to operate the trains. So slip carriages were used more and more as ordinary composite coaches which needed no separate guards, and former slips were replaced by stops.

Resuming slipping when peace returned was not a main priority on any railway. In the first place, average express speeds had to remain slow for a while because track maintenance had fallen into arrears and the time lost through stops mattered less. Secondly, there was a labour shortage until demobilisation was complete, aggravated by the fact that many former employees never came back at all, having either been killed in action or severely injured. There were also, in the minds of the Directors of the pre-War companies, doubts as to whether the Government, which had assumed control of the railways for the duration of the conflict, would return them to their former owners with adequate compensation for the damage that had resulted from four years of inadequate maintenance - or, as many expected, would nationalise them outright.

By 1922 the pattern was clear. There were to be forced amalgamations into four separate companies. Of these the Great Western, largely unchanged except for having a few smaller Welsh lines added to its system, and still retaining its former name, suffered least upheaval. In the others, and especially in the London, Midland and Scottish, there were internal strains and stresses which took time to resolve.

Possibly all this had something to do with the fact that while, during the following decade, the practice of slipping built up again on the GWR, it disappeared completely from the lines that made up the LMS system, and lessened greatly on those which united to form the LNER; of these, the Great Eastern, which had had such a long tradition of slip coach usage, returned to the practice in a small way, while the Great Central did a certain amount of experimentation. More is said below regarding these two lines.

South of the Thames the pattern was different on each of the three railways which united to form the SR. The London and South Western had ceased slipping carriages in 1902 and continued not to do so. The South Eastern and Chatham returned to the practice rather half-heartedly, and continued to be the only line which went in for Sunday slips. The London Brighton and South Coast, on which slipping had persisted throughout the War, showed signs of returning to it in a big way; by 1922, of the 24 slips it had made 10 years earlier 18 had returned. However, with the change of ownership came a change of policy which spelt the end of slipping. Progressive main line electrification was decided upon, which promised faster and more frequent services. So the LB&SCR, now the Central Section of the SR, was soon back to its 1918 figure, and after April 1932 there were no slips left at all.

On the LNER, slipping just managed to survive on the former GER lines that radiated from Liverpool Street almost until the outbreak of World War II, two detachments being made in some years, three in others, though not always at the same places. Waltham Cross had a slip service until June 1937, and Mark's Tey until 1939.

The post-War history of slipping on the main line from Marylebone, both in GCR and LNER days, makes an interesting study. The Great Central, in the days of its independent existence, was always prepared to consider innovations which promised to increase its revenue, which had never been adequate for the enrichment of its shareholders since the days of the expensive London Extension. One town in the West Midlands, well inside GWR territory, was actually nearer by rail to Marylebone than to Paddington, and the pre-War GCR had attempted to force an entry. This was Stratford-upon-Avon. Before 1914 the company had run through coaches there from London, and one of these was slipped at Woodford and then proceeded along the single track of the Stratford-on-Avon and Midland Junction Railway to that line's insignificant terminal station. In 1914 this service was provided by the 6.20 pm Bradford express from Marylebone. The War having ended, it was re-introduced on the same train. It was not, however, the GCR's first post-War slip, since from May 1920 to September 1921 a carriage was slipped at Brackley, again from the 6.20 pm, in an attempt to attract passenger patronage in that town. Its discontinuance seems to have been in part due to lack of custom; Brackley was a small place and beyond the London commuter boundary. But there may have been another reason. The slipping point had to be somewhere on a lengthy brick viaduct which crossed the upper Ouse, and if anything had gone wrong in darkness and bad weather the safety of passengers might have been put at risk. So the slip was again made at Woodford instead.

It was not the only one to be made from this train. Right at the end of the GCR's separate existence, in November 1922, one was established at the small wayside station of Finmere. Two things contributed to this. One was the accidental clustering of the residences of prominent persons who lived not far from Finmere station and who made a habit of travelling up to and back from London together on weekdays, and got to know each other, so that they formed a sort of travelling club. Among these worthies was a member of the Board of the GCR, and later of the LNER, and it may well have been he who pressed for a more convenient journey home for himself and his friends. The other favouring event was the establishing of Stowe Public School a short distance away, whose staff and scholars provided potential patronage. Thus both first and third class passengers were available to occupy a single slip coach. For 13 years, therefore, the LNER added two coaches to the 6.20 pm from Marylebone, one for Finmere and one for Woodford. The reasons for these two slips' eventual discontinuance are given in a later chapter.

From the mid-1930s until the outbreak of World War II, apart from two LNER slips at Mark's Tey and Waltham Cross, only the GWR continued the practice. As the figures cited at the beginning of this chapter show, this company had shown quite a considerable recovery until the end of the 1920s. The adjacent table shows the incidence of slipping on the GWR in 1922 just before the Grouping, ten years later in 1932, and in 1938, the last complete year of the inter-War period. The 'Cornish Riviera Express' had once more begun to slip three portions, at Westbury, Taunton and Exeter, usually but not invariably of two coaches.

Table Ten
Slip Detachments on the Great Western Railway in 1922, 1932 and 1938

Place	1922	1932	1938	Comments
Banbury	3	3	2	One 1938 slip, from High Wycombe to Banbury, provided a station-to-station average of over 60 mph.
Bath	2	1	-	All provided Paddington-Bath averages of over 60 mph.
Bicester	2	1	2	All proceeded all-stations to Banbury.
Bridgwater	1	-	-	
Chippenham	1	1	-	
Didcot	1	1	2	These slips went on to Oxford. Those of 1932 and 1938 were booked from Paddington at over 60 mph averages.
Stoke Gifford	-	1	2	For Bristol (Temple Meads) off Fishguard boat expresses. In 1938 one went on to Taunton, the other to Weston-super-Mare.
Kingham	1	-	-	This portion went through to Cheltenham by the North Cotswold line.
Leamington Spa	1	1	1	
Moreton-in-Marsh	1	-	-	Continued all-stations to Worcester.
Newbury	1	-	-	

GREAT WESTERN RAILWAY.

Slipping Coaches at Stoke Gifford.

Commencing TUESDAY, MAY 22nd, 1923.

On week-days, commencing **Tuesday, May 22nd,** the 8.45 a.m. and 8.0 p.m. trains from Paddington to Fishguard Harbour will slip coaches for Bristol at Stoke Gifford at 10.48 a.m. and 10.2 p.m. respectively.

The coaches will be slipped when passing over the underbridge between $110\frac{3}{4}$ m.p. and 111 m.p. between Winterbourne and Stoke Gifford East Box, approximately half-a-mile from Stoke Gifford East Down Inner Home Signal, and must be brought to a stand just **before reaching** that signal.

The engine and coaches for Bristol to which the coaches slipped from the London train have to be attached must be standing in readiness on the Down Goods Loop Line at Stoke Gifford East. When the coaches slipped from the London-Fishguard train have come to a stand at the Down Inner Home Signal the engine and coaches standing on the Down Goods Loop Line must set back on to them, and the train when ready to leave must proceed to Bristol over the Down Main Line.

The standard instructions for slip carriage working shewn on pages 93-102 of the General Appendix to the Book of Rules and Regulations must be observed. Special attention is directed to Clauses 24 and 25 of those instructions.

The empty trains from Dr. Day's Bridge to Stoke Gifford, and the trains taking forward the coaches slipped from the London trains as shewn above, will run as under :—

	Arr. A.M.	Dep. A.M.	Arr. P.M.	Dep. P.M.
Dr. Day's Bridge	—	A 9†35	—	9†20 B
Stapleton Road	9/38		9/23	
Filton Junction	9/47		9/32	
Stoke Gifford West	9/49		9/34	
Stoke Gifford East	9†50	—	9†35	—

A Set No. 210.　　　B Brake-third.

	Arr. A.M.	Dep. A.M.	Arr. P.M.	Dep. P.M.
Stoke Gifford East	—	10 52	—	10 7
Stoke Gifford West	10/53		10/ 8	
Filton Junction Station	10/55		10/10	
Stapleton Road	S 10/59W		10 14 SW	10 15 D
Temple Meads	11 3 C 11 15		10 20 E	—

C To form 11.15 a.m. Temple Meads to Weston-super-Mare.
D Precede 6.55 p.m. ex Swansea from Dr. Day's Bridge Junction.
E Empty train to go to Dr. Day's Bridge.

10.45 a.m. Clifton Down to Temple Meads.
To run to Old Station at Temple Meads.

10.5 p.m. Workmen's Train, Stoke Gifford to St. Philip's Marsh.
To run 5 minutes later throughout.

All concerned to note and arrange.

H. R. GRIFFITHS,
Divisional Superintendent.

Divisional Superintendent's Office,
　Bristol, May 19th, 1923.

(300)　　　　J. W. Arrowsmith Ltd., Printers, Quay Street, Bristol.

Place	1922	1932	1938	Comments
Princes Risborough	1	1	1	Continued all-stations to Banbury.
Reading	9	6	7	All from up trains.
Swindon	1	1	-	
Taplow	2	2	1	
Twyford	2	-	-	Continued to Henley-on-Thames.
Westbury	3	2	2	
Yatton	-	2	1	In 1938, Saturdays only.

Some places were no longer favoured as before. Slough lost its slips altogether, as also did Wantage Road, Savernake, Patney, Carmarthen, Hatton, Knowle and Wellington. Bridgwater had only one left from its former four. But there were some new slip services on offer - at Yatton for the Clevedon branch, and more importantly from South Wales trains for Bristol and beyond. Since the opening of the Severn Tunnel expresses from London to Cardiff, Swansea and beyond had passed within five miles of Bristol. In the up direction these trains were a difficult assignment, even for 'Castle' class 4-6-0s, because of the long pull-up from the depths of the tunnel to Patchway followed by an easier but still tiring ascent to the crest of the Cotswolds at Badminton, but in the down direction the road was easier and an extra coach or two did not matter. As early as 1923 the morning and evening trains for Fishguard Harbour, after calling at Reading, slipped a portion at Stoke Gifford for Bristol, providing a late evening service from Paddington to that city and a morning one which continued to Weston-super-Mare.

Seven slips were still being made as late as 1938 from up trains at Reading because of its importance as a junction; indeed, it was permissible to travel from the West of England to Oxford by using a Reading slip coach, though this was less direct than the route through Swindon and Didcot. The Reading detachments were rather a special case so far as operating procedure was concerned. An up train passing through that station, if it had a portion to be slipped, could not take the fast through line but had to slacken speed and use the platform road; the slip coach was then set free as soon as it was abreast of the west end platform ramp and slowed to a stop further along the platform, from which an observer could watch the whole operation. The celebrated railway photographer M.W. Earley took a sequence of photographs, reproduced in this book, showing the different stages of a Reading slip as performed in BR days.

All lines in Great Britain were affected by World War II, and slipping ceased entirely on the GWR for a while. In 1946 it began to return, five being timetabled on that line daily, using the latest slip vehicles built during the 1930s together with one of Churchward's 'Concertina' slip coaches built 30 years earlier. The number built up a little and then declined again. The last slip was made at Bicester on 10th September, 1960. (The last multiple slip (two coaches) took place at Didcot from the 7.00 am Weston-Super-Mare to Paddington on 7th June, 1960.) The occasion does not seem to have been marked in any special way and it is unlikely that the passengers realised that, negatively speaking, they were making history. A hundred and two years had seen the slip coach's rise and fall.

A portion being slipped at Bath from a London to Bristol express during the 1920s. The slip coach is one of Churchward's 'Concertina' type. *Railway Magazine*

GWR 'Toplight' slip coach No. 7109 built by Churchward in 1909.

J.H. Russell Collection

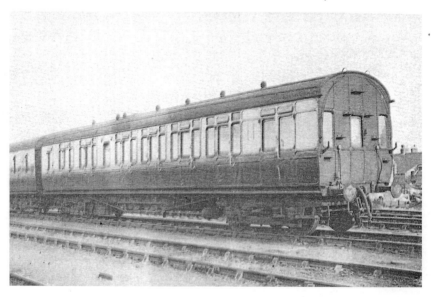

GWR 'Toplight' slip coach No. 7109 from the other side. It is seen here in BR livery.
J.H. Russell Collection

Additional vacuum cylinders under coach No. 7109.   *J.H. Russell Collection*

The following sequence of photographs was taken by the railway photographer, the late Maurice Earley, at Reading at some time early in BR days, to show the series of operations involved in slipping a coach from an up Bristol express. In this view the signals on the up main platform are set at 'all-clear' for the passage of the express through the platform road. The yellow distant signal indicates that the starting signal at the far end of the platform is also at 'all-clear' for the main train.

National Railway Museum

The express itself passing Southcote Junction shortly before the slip is to be made, with the slip coach in the rear, still in GWR chocolate and cream livery and with the GWR crest midway along its waist. It was one of the last batch of slip carriages built at Swindon in December 1938. The white disc and red light are prominent at the rear. *National Railway Museum*

The slip is made just before the rear of the train reaches the platform end at Reading.

National Railway Museum

The guard of the main train makes an acknowledging gesture to the slip-guard to show that he knows the slip has been made.

The slip coach has come to a standstill further along the platform and passengers have alighted. The severed brake pipe and steam heating pipe still hang loose, but the drawhook has now been raised and the bolt replaced over it.

National Railway Museum

A side view at the same place showing the details more clearly.

National Railway Museum

The interior of the slip's guard compartment, showing the slip-bolt handle, hand-brake handle and front window opened by a leather strap.   *National Railway Museum*

Chapter Five

Slipping in Ireland:
1895-1940

The first occasion when coaches were slipped in Ireland was 37 years after the first slip in England, and the last was 20 years earlier than the last English one. Proportionately, too, there were always far fewer - 12 daily in 1914 as against nearly 200 in England, Wales and Scotland. Curiously, however, the number remained unchanged (in the timetables, at any rate) during World War I, whereas in Great Britain it fell to only seven. The general picture is of a rather half-hearted commitment to the practice, which is understandable when one considers the different parts the railways played in society in both countries.

Not until post-World War I times did any Irish railway try to run any really fast trains. Ireland was in the main an agricultural and pastoral country with no heavy industries except in the Belfast area; there was not much demand for business travel; most people 'stayed put'. Only two main lines were double-tracked - from Dublin to Belfast and to Cork. From Dublin to Sligo, Westport, Galway, Waterford and Wexford the routes were mostly single track, with the consequent need for slow running overall to allow the exchange of tokens at passing loops. There was little need to provide slip services when trains could stop instead without losing very much time. Introducing a slip service had to be the result of careful calculation in which potential gain was weighed against possible loss.

Slip detachment first began in Ulster in 1893 in a short-lived experiment after a number of brake coaches were adapted for the purpose. The summer service between Belfast (York Road) and Coleraine/Portrush included four slips from two down trains and one up train, at Ballyclare Junction, Cookstown and Ballymoney (one in each direction at the latter) and an additional down one on Saturdays, also at Ballymoney. The experiment lasted for a year and a half, but evidently the extra revenue obtained failed to cover the additional costs, so that at the end of 1894 the practice was abandoned for a while, re-appearing at Antrim, Cookstown and Ballyclare Junction in 1897 and after, though not with yearly regularity.

The next line to operate slip services was the Great Northern of Ireland, which in 1896 began to slip a portion at Malahide, only nine miles from its Amiens Street terminus at Dublin, off an evening train for Belfast, for the benefit of commuters. A year later the coastal communities of Skerries and Balbriggan took turns at receiving them. These slips continued until 1910, the slipped carriages being all six-wheelers. In 1913 the afternoon express from Dublin to Belfast began to slip a coach at Drogheda instead of calling there; this continued throughout the War and into the 1930s, with a brief cancellation towards the War's end.

Slipping did not begin on the Great Southern and Western Railway (GS&WR) until 1901. In that year a coach was slipped daily at Kildare from the early morning Limited Mail from Dublin (Kingsbridge) to Cork. Later in the same year the 10 am and 4 pm expresses from Dublin to Cork also had slip portions attached, to be dropped off at Limerick Junction and continuing to Limerick, while the 6.10 pm for Cork slipped a portion at Portarlington for Tullamore and Athlone. The Limerick Junction slips being insufficiently patronised, they were withdrawn at the beginning of the following November, and the vehicles were used, with others, on an up slip at the same station from the 12.35 pm from Cork to Dublin, the 9.15 am from Dublin to Cork which slipped at both Kildare and Ballybrophy and then continued to Limerick by the loop line through Nenagh, and the 6.10 pm from Dublin which slipped at Sallins for Tullow.

The following year a very unusual slip service was introduced. It was not made on any main line, but on the track of the former Waterford and Central Ireland (W&CIR) line. I quote from an article in the Journal of the Irish Railway Record Society:

> The track [of the W&CIR] extended from Waterford to Mountmellick and gained access to Maryborough* by a short-spur at Conniberry Junction. Since the spur faced towards Waterford, trains between Maryborough and Mountmellick had to reverse at the Junction. Early in 1902 the morning trains from Maryborough to Mountmellick and to Waterford were combined and re-scheduled to leave Maryborough as one train at 8.15 am. Two minutes later, as the train was passing Conniberry Junction, the carriages for Mountmellick were slipped, and then taken to their destination by a locomotive which had been engaged in shunting in the goods yard at Conniberry. The same procedure was followed by the afternoon trains; these were combined into one train, which departed from Maryborough at 4.45 pm. The slip workings at Conniberry continued to operate until the 1914-1918 War.†

Here, it appears, were two slip portions which each remained attached to its parent train for a mere two minutes!

The pattern of slip-working had now more or less established itself on the GS&WR for the next 16 years. As well as the Conniberry Junction slips there were always between six and seven daily on the main line, all in the down direction, all the chief junction stations being served with the exception of Goold's Cross (for Cashel) as far as Limerick Junction. The picture in the peak year of 1913 was as follows:

Sallins	1	From the 6.15 pm from Dublin
Kildare	1	From the 6.40 am Mail from Dublin
Portarlington	2	From the 9.15 am and 3.50 pm from Dublin
Ballybrophy	2	From the same pair of trains
Thurles	1	From the 6.40 am Mail from Dublin
Conniberry Junction	2	From the 8.15 am and 4.45 pm from Maryborough to Waterford.

During the previous year the 5.15 am from Dublin had also slipped a portion at Maryborough. In 1918, however, the exigencies of the War caused all but the two slips at Ballybrophy to be discontinued.

On the Belfast & County Down Railway (B&CDR) a slip service was provided on Saturdays only from the so-called 'Golfers' Express' from November 1902 at Comber Junction, for Donaghadee; running non-stop from Comber, it reached Donaghadee in only 40 minutes from Belfast. It was established in response to

---

* Now re-named Portlaoise.

† Journal of the IRRS: Oct. 1994. Article by D.B. McNeill.

a special request from Donaghadee Golf Club, and surprisingly continued almost to the end of World War I, being discontinued in April 1918.

On the Midland Great Western Railway slipping began at Enfield in 1909, on the main line from Dublin to Mullingar and Galway. Until that year the company had had no locomotives which could be relied upon to run for 50 miles without a stop for water, so that a halt at Enfield had been necessary in any case; here passengers could change into the branch line train for Edenderry. However, in 1909 new engines appeared which could manage a non-stop run from Dublin (Broadstone) to Mullingar without the need to refill their tender tanks, so a slip was made at Enfield which then continued to Edenderry. During the summer of 1909 this slip, from the 4.50 pm from Dublin, was supplemented by a summer-only one from the 8.45 am. This pattern continued till the outbreak of World War I, when both were suspended; one returned soon after the ending of hostilities. For a short while, also, during the summer of 1918, a slip service was provided to serve Cavan, when the 3.05 pm from Mullingar to Sligo slipped a portion at Inny Junction, 10 miles beyond Mullingar, which was then taken on to Cavan by a locomotive that had run light from Mullingar to Inny half an hour earlier.

Exactly why this slip should have been made is not clear; the engine could have been coupled to the coach at Mullingar instead of Inny. In any case it only lasted during that summer.

The events in Ireland which affected train services adversely were not so much World War I itself as the 'Troubles' attendant on the struggles for independence from Britain and the subsequent Civil War between the Free State government established in 1922 and the dissidents who would not accept the settlement reached in that year. During this period, while slip services were advertised during 1920-1921, they were probably either not made at all or only made occasionally. Between 1922 and 1924 none was even advertised. In 1925, after all the lines that served places in the Republic but not beyond the Border had been amalgamated into the Great Southern Railway, slip services were once again notified in the public timetables, beginning with one at Kildare for Waterford. During 1926-1928 one was also made at Portarlington. The Kildare slip continued until 1940, by which time it was the only one left in the Republic. Then the 'Emergency' (as World War II was termed in Ireland) affected all the train services because of the shortage of coal; slipping ended altogether and was never revived.

On the Great Northern Railway of Ireland the practice was advertised to re-commence in the summer of 1921 with detachments from the 3 pm and 6.35 pm Dublin-Belfast expresses at Drogheda at 3.36 and 7.11 respectively, the main trains running non-stop to Dundalk. In 1923, however, the evening train stopped at Drogheda instead of slipping. A slip was also advertised at Goraghwood from the evening train during 1921-1922. In 1926, after the Border had been established, the now-discontinued slip at Goraghwood was replaced by a stop for Customs examination. This station, however, did see a slip in the opposite direction from the evening Belfast-Dublin Mail, which was taken on to Warrenpoint, during most but not all the years from 1926 to 1940. Also, an interesting through-service slip was established, during the summer months only, at Lisburn from 1921-1933 and 1936-1940, from the 9 am from Dublin to Belfast, which then proceeded along the branch to Antrim, avoiding Belfast altogether, before joining the Northern Counties Committee (NCC) line to Coleraine and Portrush.

No slips were introduced or re-introduced on the NCC or B&CDR after World War I. In the Republic the slip at Enfield was re-introduced for a short while, being transferred from the 1.10 pm from Dublin to Galway and Sligo.

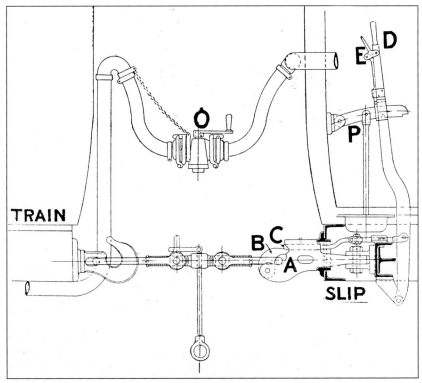

Slip Mechanism used on the GWR

A   Slip coach drawhook.
B   Hinged part of drawhook, opening forwards.
C   Bolt which, when drawn back, allows hook to open.
D   Handle for withdrawing bolt.
E   Handle for loosening ratchet catch on rachet 'P'.
O   Slip cock on brake pipe junction.

Chapter Six

Slip Detachment Procedure

Having passed under review the general picture of slip coach use, its origin, rise, decline and eventual disappearance, one should now pause to consider the methods, machinery and cautionary practices that were needed, looking first at the design of the carriage itself, then at the on-train preparation, then at the handling of the detachable portion by the staff involved until the intended platform was reached, including the emergency provisions in case anything prevented the slip from being made.

In regard to the vehicle, it was usual to design one that could convey all classes of passenger - though this was not a necessity if the whole portion to be slipped comprised two or more coaches. In the early 20th century most companies had discontinued offering second class accommodation on any of their trains, though the South Eastern and Chatham was a notable exception, as I personally recall from being occasionally carried in a second class compartment during the early 1920s when travelling from Tonbridge to Tunbridge Wells. A typical slip carriage had a smallish guard's compartment at one or both ends; if the latter, this made possible its use as a slip vehicle in whichever direction it was travelling. The GWR, the most considerable user of slip vehicles, built most of them with a guard's compartment and slip gear at each end, losing a few passenger seats but making the use of a turntable unnecessary if the coach was rostered to be slipped on the return as well as on the outward journey.

If long-distance working was envisaged - for example, from Paddington to Bath in contrast to Paddington to Slough, access to a toilet compartment would also be provided, often along a side corridor. Additional coaches added to the slip coach could of course be ordinary ones, with or without side corridors, according to requirements.

Not all slip carriages were originally designed as such. It was sometimes deemed more economical to modify an existing third class brake vehicle, the GER and some other lines did this. The disadvantage would be, if that coach alone were to be slipped, that there would be more luggage space than was necessary; this would matter less, however, if the slip portion consisted of several vehicles, as was often the case on the latter line.

On-train preparation began when the slip portion was marshalled to the rest of the main train. There was a good deal more to this than the actual coupling-on. The rear end of the slip portion had to be distinguished by special lamps specially arranged. New guidelines introduced in 1897 by the Railway Clearing House specified that if there was only one slip portion it had to carry a red and a white light between the two rear red tail lamps, one above the other. If there were two slips to be made, the first to be detached was thus marked, while the last had to carry a red light *beside* a white light. When for a while the 'Cornish Riviera Express' took three slip portions out of Paddington, the second to be detached, at Taunton, carried a triangle of three red lamps. Each lamp was encircled by a disc of the same colour, for easy daytime sighting. Thus

Flashlight photograph (taken c. 1905) of the interior of a GER slip guard's compartment. The lever operating the bolt on the slip coupling is seen on the left; to the right of it is the gauge showing the pressure in the Westinghouse brake cylinder; partly visible is the guard's brake handle in the foreground.
Railway Magazine

The slip guard operating the lever which loosens the draw hook to effect the slip; immediately afterwards he will rotate the brake handle to enable the slip carriage to move quickly away from the main train.   *GWR Museum, Swindon*

signalmen could observe, as the train passed their boxes, whether or not it was as complete as it should be at that point in its journey.

The slip guard had also to satisfy himself that the slipping apparatus was functioning properly. His last opportunity to do this would be at the last stopping station before the slip took effect, but he would more usually do this when he joined the train at its point of origin if the intermediate stop or stops were brief ones. He had also to make sure that the warning bell or horn at the front of the slip carriage was in order and would not fail to sound when necessary. In the case of the 'corridor slips' briefly used on the LNWR in 1914, the sealing-off mechanism on the vestibule connection had also to be checked.

These precautions having been taken, the train was free to leave. From then onwards the slip coach guard had the same responsibility for the slip portion and its passengers as did his counterpart on the main train - which might be almost as great if the portion were several coaches in length, as with the slips for Hertford at Broxbourne. When the moment for slipping approached he needed to be on the *qui vive* for the appropriate point at which his special duties began. He had to bear in mind the weather conditions. On a very misty day, or when the rails were wet and slippery, it was for him to estimate whether slipping might be inadvisable, since the first would make observation difficult while the second would affect his ability to brake the slip portion with the means at his disposal. Should he decide against making the slip, he would give a signal to the driver to that effect when the latter looked back along the train, as the regulations required him to do when the expected moment of detachment was imminent. A red flag waved, or a red lamp swung from side to side, would warn the driver to halt the whole train at the platform so that the slip portion could be detached by hand; the main train could then re-start and go on its way after a delay costing between five and ten minutes. If, however, the guard did not wish to slip, but found that he could not make visual contact with the driver, he would apply the hand brake in his slip compartment firmly enough to slow the whole train down, thereby alerting the driver to the need to stop.

Conversely, either the driver or the station master at the station where the slip was to be made could decide that the slip was inadvisable. The former might have found that an adverse signal or a permanent way check obliged him to reduce speed, so depriving the slip portion of much of the impetus it would need to reach the platform. In this case he would apply the engine's and train's brakes and this would alert the slip guard, who would then refrain from slipping. The local station master, on the other hand, was the one best placed to assess the weather, and he could veto the slip by instructing the signalman to set the signals at danger. As the slip guard was under instruction never to effect a slip if the signals were against the train, this too would cancel the slip.

Guards were strictly instructed that if the slipping mechanism failed to work when first operated there should be no second attempt; the driver was to be given the signal to stop by means of a firm brake application. Yet another reason for not slipping might be the excessive weight of the slip portion. If all the latter's seats were taken and there were also several standing passengers it would be more difficult to control the deceleration with the braking power at the guard's disposal. Here again it was for the slip guard to use a sensible discretion.

Slip compartment end of a slip carriage on the Lancashire & Yorkshire Railway, as used on the Leeds-Liverpool trains which slipped coaches at Rochdale pre-World War I. Note the hinged slip hook, sand pipe for assisting in braking when the rail was wet, and the warning hooter pointing to one side at the lower right-hand corner. The notice above the left-hand buffer says 'WHEN THIS SLIP VAN IS IN SERVICE AS AN ORDINARY VAN THE VAN SCREW SHACKLE MUST BE USED FOR COUPLING NOT THE SLIP HOOK'.

National Railway Museum

View of the interior of slip guard's compartment in a L&YR slip carriage in 1913. Handbrake worked by wheel with handle. The slipping lever is below the central window. The darkish cord with the loop at the end operates the brake closure lever on the brake pipe outside. The vacuum brake lever is below the right-hand window. Note the gauge showing degree of vacuum. The foot pedal (*to the right*) sounds the warning bell. *National Railway Museum*

Slip guard's compartment in a Churchward slip carriage in 1927. Note the ratchet loosening lever on the slip coupling detachment handle. *GWR Museum, Swindon*

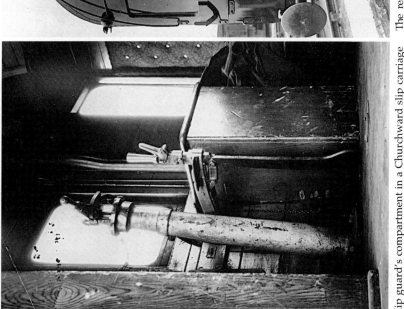

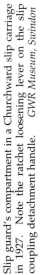

The rear end of one of Collett's three slip coaches built at Swindon in 1929 for use on the 'Cornish Riviera Express', in brand new condition. Note especially the brake pipe leading upwards to where it enters the slip compartment about 3 feet above the floor, and the lever at its upper end which can be actuated by pulling the alarm chain in one of the compartments, thus lessening the vacuum and applying the brakes.

GWR Museum, Swindon

If it were considered safe to slip, the necessary apparatus was put into action. One may first describe the method used on the GWR, differences on other lines being touched on later. An article in the *Great Western Railway Magazine* for January 1907 describes the operation simply and straightforwardly, and it seems best to reproduce what the writer, E.S. Hadley, had to say.

> The apparatus . . . is quite simple. A hook on the front vehicle of those to be detached, to which is linked the coupling chain of the main portion of the train, is so constructed that the upper half of it, which is held in the closed position by a bolt, works at a joint when the bolt is withdrawn, opens outwards . . . and allows the coupling link to be drawn out, thus parting the coaches. The bolt is worked by a lever in the guard's compartment at the front end of the slip portion.
>
> Most important of the operations for slipping vehicles are those to prevent a severance of the vacuum automatic brake connections between the main and slip portions of the train until the continuous pipe on each portion has been stopped to prevent an inrush of air which would bring the whole train to a stand. A stop cock, known as the slip cock, is attached between the flexible pipes of the two portions, and upon turning the slip cock handle . . . the vacuum in the main train is sealed. This handle is within the reach of the guard of the slip portion, who leans out of the window at the end of his compartment to turn it.
>
> In an open case in the slip guard's compartment is an indicator connected with the vacuum brake apparatus, which shows the words WRONG TO SLIP until the vacuum in the slip portion is sealed. This is done by turning a handle, when the word RIGHT appears in place of WRONG. This done, the guard uncouples by hand the flexible pipe of the slip portion from the slip cock, the latter of course remaining attached to the pipe on the main portion of the train. The slip cock, when thus uncoupled, is held up by a chain to prevent its striking against the end of the carriage.
>
> Whilst the words WRONG TO SLIP appear at the indicator, the lever which operates the bolt on the slip hook is held fast by a lock, so that the bolt cannot be withdrawn. The sealing of the vacuum in the slip portion releases the lock, and the guard is able to work the lever to detach the vehicles. The vacuum brake remains available for use on the slip portion, but it must not be employed, except in case of emergency when the hand-brake power would be insufficient.*
>
> Before slipping takes place the guard in the slip portion must apply the hand brake slightly to the wheels of his van, and put it on more forcibly immediately he has withdrawn the bolt from the slip hook. The main portion of the train will then draw away from the slip portion. The brake must afterwards be released, but should be applied again if necessary to maintain a sufficient interval between the two portions to enable the slip portion to be stopped clear of the main train, should the latter slacken speed or stop for any reason before reaching the platform.†
>
> The distance from the platform that slip vehicles are to be detached from the train depends upon the gradient of the line, the weight of the slip portion, the speed of the train and other conditions. If the line is not clear for the main portion of the train to run

---

* The reason for the prohibition was that there was no means of restoring the vacuum within the slip coach after the brake pipe had been sealed. The GWR and some other companies, though keeping the same rule about using the hand brake only, did after the time this article was written add additional reservoirs to slip coaches, so that in an emergency the guard had more brake power at his disposal. The vacuum brake was more effective than the hand brake, if it did need to be used, because it worked on all the wheels of the slip portion, not on those of the leading bogie alone. Some time after the fitting of additional reservoirs it was permitted to use it, apart from emergencies, for up to three applications.

† In later days, following the addition of extra vacuum reservoirs, after the slip portion had drawn clear of the main train the slipping lever was returned to a middle position which connected the vacuum brake to these reservoirs, so that three more full vacuum brake applications were rendered possible.

at the usual speed through the station at which slipping should take place, the slip portion must not be detached while travelling, but the train must stop at the platform for this to be done. The guard responsible for slipping must, on approaching the station, look out for the fixed signals and refrain from slipping unless the distant signal is at 'all right' and the usual speed of the train is maintained.

Not all railways, of course, used the vacuum brake, as the GWR did; some employed the Westinghouse system, in which compressed air kept the train's brakes in the 'off' position. However, the operation of sealing the brake pipe was the same, so far as the slip guard was concerned, his closure of the cock preventing not an inrush but an outrush of air.

The article above refers to the situation as it was in 1907, and omits to mention the steam-heating pipe, which by that time was in customary use. Trains were heated in cold weather by convection heaters beneath the seats in the compartments, which received steam from the locomotive along a continuous series of pipes that stretched the length of the train. In earlier days the slip portions, like the trains they were attached to, had been unheated, and chilly passengers had to get what comfort they could from hired foot-warmers. When steam heating began it was at first supplied to slip portions only as far as the last stopping station before the slip - which of course in many cases meant not at all after the departure from the terminus. This could obviously deter people from using a slip portion at all if the weather were cold. However, means were eventually found of connecting the steam pipe of the main train to that of the slip portion by a joint that sealed itself automatically when pulled apart, and this was already the practice on the GWR when the above description was written.

Once the slip had been effected the detached portion became in effect a separate train, the slip guard being now the 'driver' with this difference, that he could only slow the portion down and had no means of making it continue to move. He would need to be familiar with the changes in gradient and curvature, and how to apply his hand brake in such a manner that a smooth gradual deceleration brought his coach to a halt at the right place at the station platform. (How difficult this might be can be seen in the case of the slips at Accrington, referred to in Chapter Three above.)

GWR slips and those on some other railways were made using hinged draw-hooks which opened forwards; the diagram on page 56 indicates the manner of operation. Another arrangement, used on the Great Central Railway and some other lines, was an earlier method in which the slip carriage's shackle, not its hook, was made to open when the guard pulled a cord in his compartment - again, see the captioned diagram. At the time of the slip carriage accident (*see Chapter Eight*) at Woodford on the main line of the former GCR this older method was still being employed.

Colonel Woodhouse, in his Report to the Ministry of Transport regarding the accident, described the procedure as follows:

The equipment used for slipping on this section of the line comprises a special pattern of screw coupling and special connections for the steam heating pipe and for the train pipe of the vacuum brake. The slip coach itself has a draw hook of the usual pattern, but is provided with a screw coupling having an outer shackle with a hinged end secured by a spring latch; this shackle is placed on a draw hook at the rear of the main portion of the train. The guard in charge of the slip coach travels in the brake compartment at its leading end, which has end windows; when he desires he can operate the latch by means of a cord, so allowing the shackle to open and releasing the draw hook.*

The disadvantage of the 'Rope Release' method was the length of cord needed. The cord, after leaving the point of attachment to the sleeve on the shackle, passed under a pulley, rope upwards to an orifice in the front of the slip coach and hung down inside the slip guard's compartment. There was a good deal of slack, and in a strong wind this loose cord could vibrate and possibly get caught on a metal projection from one of the brake hose fittings. After the Woodford accident no further slips were made on former GCR metals. The Great Southern Railway of Ireland, however, continued to employ this method until 1940, after which slipping on that line was discontinued. The Caledonian, during the years up to 1914 when it slipped carriages, also used a rope to release the hinged end of the shackle, but in this case the releasing pull was not round a pulley upwards but longitudinal, the release cord entering the guard's compartment at floor level.

Some means of audible warning was needed at the front end of a slip carriage. During its short journey to the stop at the platform it made no noise but the rolling of its wheels, so that anyone working on the line needed to be made aware of its approach and realise that, though the main train had gone by, it was not yet safe

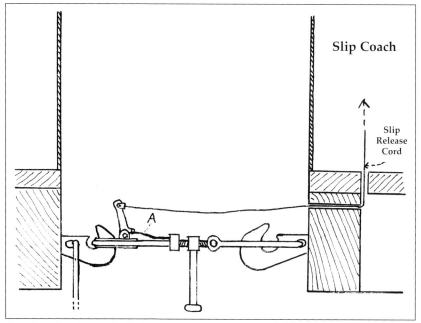

Drawing showing method of 'rope release' as used on the Caledonian Railway. The shackle over the draw hook on the last coach of the main train is pulled open against the pressure of the spring 'A', which normally keeps it closed.

* Ministry of Transport Accident Report, March 1936.

to step behind it. The bell, or horn (which latter was operated through bellows) was worked by a foot pedal so that the guard could have both hands free.

Finally, a few remarks about the speed at which a slip portion might be travelling at the moment of slipping. Theoretically this might be as high as the parent train was able to travel, but in practice there was usually some deceleration first, since the detachment had to be made at some point at the lineside recognisable by the slip guard - usually a distant signal which, were it at danger (later 'caution'), would disallow the slip from being made. The highest speed recorded at the time of slipping appears to have been in 1935, when a passenger in a slip coach for Banbury at the rear of a London to Birmingham express found his train was travelling at 75 mph at the moment of detachment - a very unusual speed at this point, slip or no slip, since the train had previously had to slow at Aynho Junction and would have to do the same at Banbury. In 1910 a slip portion weighing 120 tons was recorded as being detached from a down express on the LB&SCR at the approach to Haywards Heath at 67 mph; again, this seems very much on the high side for so weighty a portion on a down gradient of 1 in 264, since only the brakes on the first coach would have been usable, unless the occasion was regarded as an emergency and the Westinghouse air brakes were used as well. When slips were made on sharply curved track the speed was always reduced first, and in such cases the slip portion might cling fairly closely to the parent train in order not to lose so much impetus that a platform stop would not be possible. This could happen at Bath from a non-stop express to Bristol, or from the 'Cornish Riviera Express' at Westbury in the days before that station could be avoided by using the by-pass line.

At Reading on slips from up trains, and also at Exeter in the case of the down 'Cornish Riviera Express' there had to be a considerable slowing for the whole train to take the platform road. At Reading, in the case of trains coming from the Westbury direction, which had already needed to reduce speed twice, at Southcote and Oxford Road junctions, the GWR installed separate small distant signals in 1946 to indicate that the platform line was clear. These were

> . . . small fish-tail arms below the home signals on the up gantry at the Main Line West box, covering both main and relief platforms. When 'off' they showed the slip guard that the platform was clear, and for some way beyond. The line of sight for slip guards on the up line at Reading was considered insufficient. The arms were operated by electric motors worked from the Main Line East box.*

The requirement to take the platform line was the consequence of a general rule made in the interests of safety, that no movement of points should ever be made between the passing of a main train and of its slip portion. This inevitably resulted in a little loss of time and in the case of the 'Cornish Riviera Express' during the periods when it slipped at Exeter, some of its drivers, who felt they needed every second they could spare if their train was running behind time, with Dainton and Rattery banks ahead of them, resented this requirement and asked for the slipping point to be on the through road, and the detached portion to be shunted to the platform, so that no slowing would be necessary; however, their representations were not successful.

---

* From a personal letter from Mr R.W. Kidner.

Chapter Seven

Slip Coach Construction

Since this book is intended to give a general picture of slip carriage use rather than an exhaustive analysis, there follows a fairly complete account of the slip vehicles employed from 1890 onwards on the railway on which most slipping took place, the Great Western, and after that such details as have been discovered about the vehicles used on other lines - the Great Eastern in particular.*

In regard to information about the Great Western Railway, I am especially grateful to Michael Harris, whose comprehensive book *Great Western Coaches: 1890-1954* provides a thorough and detailed account of all the coaching stock built at Swindon during those 65 years. From it one gains an appreciation of the gradually changing scene on that line in the period following the abolition of the broad gauge, under successive designers Dean, Churchward, Collett and Hawksworth, and of the successive alterations in style. GWR slip coaches were specialised variants of many of these types, and some of them endured into the 1950s and were used by British Railways.

The total number built during those years was 79 - though not all were in use at the same time since some of the earlier ones had been withdrawn before some of the later ones appeared. In addition, some brake composite coaches - it does not appear how many - built between 1894 and 1896 were modified to enable them too to be slipped.

Of slip coaches built or modified for use on the broad gauge no details appear now to be extant; one assumes that the main special features of later ones were found in them also - the front window allowing the guard a clear view ahead, a detachment device, whether by rope or lever, and a warning bell or horn.

Once the construction of new standard gauge vehicles had begun, with records commencing in 1890, the first new slip vehicles, six in all, were built during the following year and came out in November 1891. Others followed at irregular intervals, the last appearing in December 1938, again to a total of six, shortly before the outbreak of World War II put an end to slipping for some years. In general the types of passenger vehicles built at Swindon during these years may be grouped according to their special characteristics. Nearly all constructed between 1890 and 1904 had clerestory roofs, which allowed a little light into the upper part of each compartment as well as affording some ventilation. Dean favoured this type of roof; nevertheless it had some disadvantages, since it somewhat weakened the whole carriage structure and made internal cleaning more difficult. As soon as Churchward was firmly in the saddle at Swindon he began to build carriages with a

---

* In regard to these latter, I am particularly indebted to Mr B.D.J. Walsh, who kindly allowed me to consult the text of a talk given by him to the Railway Club in September 1992.

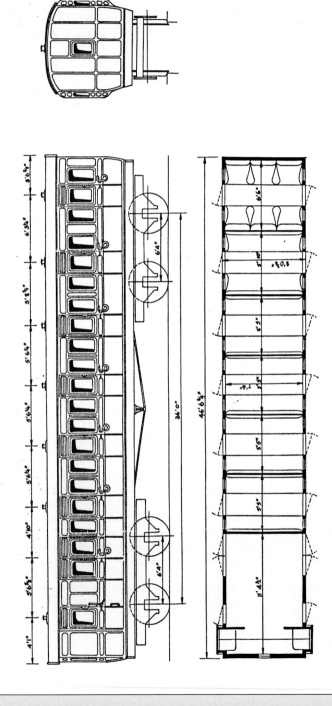

A late 19th century GWR composite brake carriage with an end window which permitted it to be adapted for slipping. *J.H. Russell Collection*

different profile; he discarded the clerestory and gave his roofs a semi-elliptical section* and this remained the practice throughout the rest of the GWR's independent existence.

For some two years Churchward produced carriages of great length, between 69 and 70 ft long and 9½ ft wide across the waist. They could have been used on no other line, but the GWR, having originally been built to the 7 ft gauge, had more room on either side after it had gone over to the standard gauge. From their massive appearance these coaches became known as 'Dreadnoughts' (the allusion being to a new type of battleship recently constructed for the British Navy).

Later, in order to maximise the interior width of his coaches, Churchward recessed the doors (because of their laterally-projecting handles) so that instead of making a straight surface the sides went in and out along;the vehicle. Such carriages were nicknamed 'concertinas' from the supposed resemblance to the bellows of an accordion. After about a year this type was discontinued, and maximising illumination rather than width became the objective; carriage windows now had 'toplights' of glass placed above them right up to the roof edge.

The building of 'Toplight' stock continued until Churchward's retirement. From 1923, under Collett, new carriages became rather shorter, though still from 9 to 9½ ft wide. Toplights disappeared and exterior surfaces became plain without mouldings; some were steel-panelled and some had 'bow ends.' After Collett's retirement Hawksworth introduced further innovations, particularly sloping off the roofs at each end to resemble Gresley's stock on the LNER.

Slip carriages appeared in clerestory, concertina, toplight and later Collett types. In addition one was built for use with a travelling Post Office train which, passing Bristol without stopping and avoiding Temple Meads station, detached a portion near Bedminster with mails for the Midlands.†

GWR slip vehicles were mostly double-ended, with two slipguard's compartments, the exceptions being four built in 1898 with clerestories and two in 1908 with toplights and elliptical roofs. The former appear to have been intended for use in pairs as a slip portion detached at Reading from an up express from Birkenhead and Birmingham to Paddington, to continue to Kent along the SE&CR's Reading to Redhill branch.

Although the last coaches actually to be built as slip vehicles were produced in 1938, 20 years later, in BR days, three of Hawksworth's brake composites (of 1948) were modified for slipping, when the end of slipping was almost in sight. It was one of these, No. 7374, which was used on the last slip to be made in Britain, at Bicester on 9th September, 1960, from the 5.10 pm from Paddington to Wolverhampton.

A list of GWR slip carriages, with details, appears below.

---

* 'Elliptical' is a rough approximation; in fact the sectional curve was essentially one of large radius, with arcs of lesser radius on either side.
† See Appendix Seven for a discussion on the GPO's use of a slip vehicle.

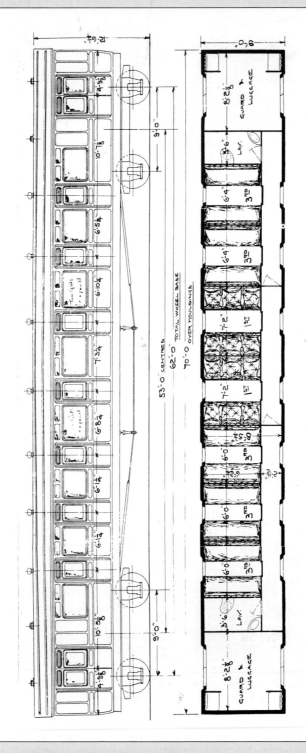

A Churchward 'Concertina' slip coach, completed in August 1905; 15 were built according to this diagram, which does not show the three windows at each end.

J.H. Russell Collection

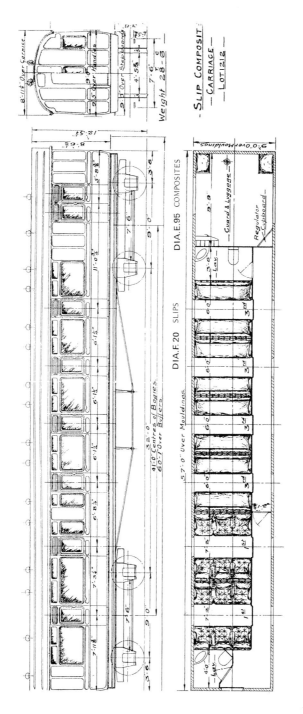

SLIP COMPOSITE
— CARRIAGE —
— LOT 1212 —

J.H. Russell Collection

DIA. E.95 COMPOSITES

DIA. F.20 SLIPS

One of three single-ended 'Toplight' slip coaches, built as brake composites and then modified in 1913. In a coach designed for slipping the guard's van would usually be much less spacious.

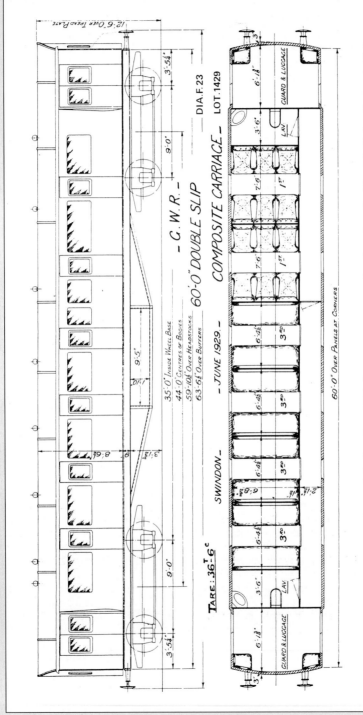

- G.W.R. -

60'-0" DOUBLE SLIP

COMPOSITE CARRIAGE

- SWINDON - - JUNE 1929. -

DIA.F.23 LOT.1429

12'-6" Over Tread Plate

35'-0" Inside Wheel Base
44'-0" Centres of Bogies
59'-0½" Over Headstocks
63'-6½" Over Buffers

60'-0" Over Panels at Corners

GUARD & LUGGAGE

LAV

TARE: 36-6ᵀᶜ

A 'bow-ended' double-ended slip coach built in June 1929; three were constructed and used on the 'Cornish Riviera Express'. Note the recessed doors in the van portions at each end. There was a warning bell at each end.

J.H. Russell Collection

Table Eleven
GWR Slip Carriage Construction

Date of completion	Number built	Type	Length	Width	Comments
28.11.1891	6	Clerestory	50 ft 0¾ in.	8 ft 0¾ in.	
1.12.1894	6	Clerestory	50 ft 0¾ in.	8 ft 0¾ in.	
26.6.1897	4	Clerestory	58 ft 0¾ in.	8 ft 6¾ in.	
31.7.1897	6	Clerestory	56 ft 0¾ in.	8 ft 6¾ in.	
30.4.1898	2	Clerestory	38 ft 6¾ in.	8 ft 6¾ in.	Single-ended
25.6.1898	2	Clerestory	38 ft 6¾ in.	8 ft 6¾ in.	Single-ended
13.7.1901	2	Clerestory	58 ft 0¾ in.	8 ft 6¾ in.	
11.7.1903	6	Clerestory	58 ft 0¾ in.	8 ft 6¾ in.	
14.1.1904	1	Post Office stowage Vehicle	68 ft	9 ft 6¾ in.	With wired glass roof & single side gangway
25.8.1906	15	Concertina	70 ft 0 in.	9 ft 0 in.	
19.9.1908	2	Toplight	57 ft 9 in.	9 ft 0 in.	
20.11.1909	14	Toplight	57 ft 9 in.	9 ft 0 in.	
28.10.1916	4	Toplight	69ft 11¼ in.	8 ft 11¼ in.	
21.12.1929	3	Bow-ended	61 ft 4½ in.	9 ft 5¾ in.	For use on 'Cornish Riviera Express'
24.12.1938	6	Bow ended	60 ft 11¼ in.	8 ft 11 in.	
1958	3	Curved roof-ends	64 ft 0 in.	8 ft 11 in.	Modified from 1948 Hawksworth brake composites

TOTAL: 82

Some information is available about slip coaches employed on the Great Eastern Railway. Except during the final months of this company's separate existence all were either four-wheeled or six-wheeled vehicles. It is not possible now to give a completely comprehensive account, since a number of the GER slip vehicles were modified brake thirds, and some of them were later re-modified to their former condition at dates which are occasionally wanting.

The first slip carriages to be specially built for this company were produced at Stratford by S.W. Johnson. These were two four-wheeled first and second class composites, each only 24 feet long. One was used on the GER's first slip service at Chelmsford, which began in 1872. Subsequently Johnson modified seven other coaches, also four-wheelers and of similar length and also first and second class composites, which had originally been built by R. Sinclair during 1859-1865. In 1877 W. Adams produced five tri-composite coaches, all four-wheelers, each 27 ft long. This made a total of 14.

In 1885 James Holden built six larger slip coaches at Stratford, each 32 ft long, tri-composite, running on six wheels and fitted with Westinghouse brake equipment, which had just been adopted by the GER as standard. In 1890 two additional similar coaches were introduced, and the aged Sinclair four-wheelers were withdrawn. So in this year the total number of slip vehicles on the GER was 23, covering 18 daily services. A little later the vehicles built by Johnson and Adams were converted back to ordinary brake composites. At about this

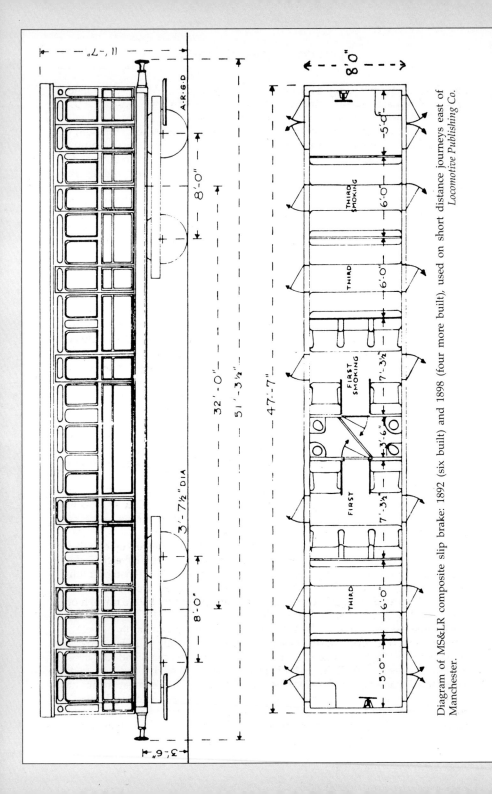

Diagram of MS&LR composite slip brake: 1892 (six built) and 1898 (four more built), used on short distance journeys east of Manchester.

Locomotive Publishing Co.

time, too, the former 'hinged shackle' slipping gear gave place to the 'hinged drawhook' type; Holden, having come from Swindon, probably considered that the method his former company used was preferable.

Next came three modified carriages, two four-wheeled brake-thirds built in 1877 and 1883, 27 ft long, and a single six-wheeled brake composite first built in 1896, which, at 34 ft 6 in. in length, was the largest coach so far to be used for this purpose on this railway. It was later to be involved in the Mark's Tey accident of December 1906, and survived after repair.

In 1912 the first of Holden's four-wheeler slip coaches was withdrawn, and no further ones were built or converted until the eve of the absorption of the GER into the LNER. Meanwhile, one by one, Holden's vehicles were either withdrawn or turned back into ordinary brake carriages. By the time of the Grouping only a few remained to be incorporated into LNER stock, and in 1923 three of these were also withdrawn. Meanwhile, however, in 1922, a number of bogie carriages which had been built as brake composites in 1910 were equipped with slip apparatus, and some were put into service on the Mark's Tey slip portion, which ran forwards after detachment to Sudbury and Bury St Edmunds. They were marked with the inscription: 'To run between London - Marks Tey - Cambridge only'. Presumably they were also used in ordinary service between Bury St Edmunds and Cambridge occasionally.

In the spring of 1932 the last of Holden's four-wheeled slip carriages was taken out of service, leaving only his large six-wheeled conversion, which was used on a slip service to Waltham Cross until 1936, when it was withdrawn, the Waltham Cross slip ending at the same time. The bogie slip vehicles still remaining continued to operate on the Mark's Tey service until the beginning of the summer timetable of 1939. The outbreak of World War II in September 1939 caused the cancellation of all slip services in Great Britain, so these vehicles were then used as ordinary brake composites until 1954, the slip gear remaining in them but not being used. They were then withdrawn.

In 1892 the Manchester, Sheffield and Lincolnshire Railway built six slip coaches in its Gorton works, and added four more in 1898. They were bogie vehicles 47 ft 7 in. long, of which 10 ft was taken up by the guard's slip compartments at either end; between these were a pair of first class compartments, each with access to a separate toilet, and flanked by one third class compartment on one side and two on the other. This gave first class passengers a very generous provision of space, with seats for 10 persons; third class passengers, with five-a-side seating and no toilet access, were less generously treated, though probably no slip coach passenger had to travel more than 50 miles. These vehicles had no side corridors.

After the London Extension had been finished, however, and a slip vehicle on a northbound train from Marylebone could travel for as long as 1¾ hours before being slipped, better accommodation was clearly needed, and the now-renamed Great Central Railway built two batches of slip carriages with toilet access for all passengers. As before there were two first class compartments and three third, but the whole vehicle was 2½ ft longer, and each end guard's compartment slightly shorter, so that room was found for a pair of third class toilets, one leading from one compartment, the other from the other two by

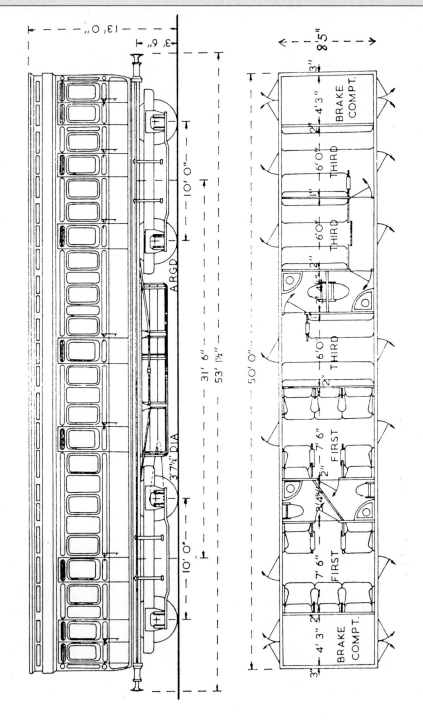

Diagram of GCR composite slip brake, 1903. Six were built by Ashbury's of Manchester for use on the London Extension.

Locomotive Publishing Co.

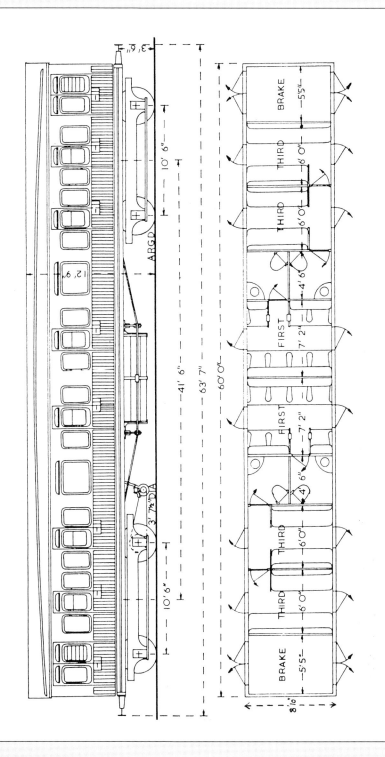

Diagram of GCR composite slip brake, 1911. Two were built to supplement the six clerestoried roof slips of 1903. Both were used for many years on the 6.20 pm from Marylebone to Bradford, being slipped at Finmere and Woodford respectively, until an accident to one caused both to be withdrawn (*see Chapter Eight*).

Locomotive Publishing Co.

means of a short side corridor. These coaches had clerestory roofs. G. Dow, in his history of the GCR, describes these vehicles in appreciative terms which I cannot forbear from quoting:

> The internal decor . . . was typical of the period. These vehicles carried 10 first and 26 third class passengers, embodied lavatories for both classes and luggage compartments, were electrically lit throughout on Stone's system and, of course, were steam-heated. The first class compartments were finished in walnut and incised with gold; the spring mattress seats, together with the backs, were covered in green cloth and stuffed with curled hair; parcel racks, umbrella racks and electroliers were in burnished brass. In the lavatories the dado and woodwork were of walnut and sycamore, and the WCs and washbasins of decorated porcelain, the floors being covered with mosaic tiles laid in cement. The finish of the third class compartments was polished oak, the spring seats being trimmed by moquette, and sliding doors gave access to the corridor. The corridors and lavatories were finished in light and dark oak, and the equipment of the lavatories was similar to those of the first class.*

Certainly an advance in comfort on the third class provision in the MS&LR slip vehicles. Their users, contemplating the decorated porcelain in the toilet compartment, might well feel they were being pampered, while the first class passenger, regarding the 'walnut incised with gold' in the woodwork, and the burnished brass electroliers, might have supposed himself to be in a smaller version of the Ritz or Claridge's.

The GCR's second batch of slip coaches, of which only two were built, though not less comfortable inside, had a quite different external appearance. They were 60 ft long, which allowed room for four instead of three third class compartments; the first class ones had four seats abreast instead of three, though the resulting narrowness of each seat was partly compensated by the slightly increased width of the coach. The roof was elliptical, not clerestory. Stone's electric lighting, dynamo-generated by means of a band from a bogie axle, was installed as before. The coach's exterior gave an impression of great strength and had vertical matchboarding beneath the windows. These two carriages were eventually incorporated in the formation of the 6.20 pm evening express from Marylebone to Bradford, being slipped one after the other at Finmere and Woodford, until an unfortunate accident in December 1935, described in the following chapter, caused both to be removed from service.

A little information has survived about the slip carriages used on the South Eastern and Chatham Railway, whose larger joint partner, the South Eastern Railway, had been one of the first companies to practise slipping in 1858. By 1900 its original enthusiasm had waned greatly, and by 1914 there were only six slips being made daily, so a large number of slip vehicles was not needed. Those built for the purpose, as well as two brake thirds which were modified as slip coaches in 1911/1912, were characteristically SE&CR in appearance, with birdcage roofs over the guard's compartments. In his book on SE&CR coaching stock D. Gould describes five built in 1909.† They were just over 50 feet long, had a slipping compartment at one end only, and a large luggage compartment with double doors on either side next to it. Then followed two first class compartments, each having seats for five passengers and access to its own toilet.

---

* G. Dow: *Great Central: Vol. III: 1900-1922*: p. 145.
† *Bogie Carriages of the South Eastern & Chatham Railway*, D. Gould, Oakwood Press, 1993.

Next came two second class compartments with 13 seats in all and access along a short corridor to a single toilet compartment right at the end of the coach. These five vehicles, with the two converted ones, sufficed for all the SE&CR slips until the practice ended soon after the company was absorbed into the Southern Railway.

Information about slip vehicles used on the Lancashire and Yorkshire Railway is necessarily incomplete because of the destruction of records by fire on more than one occasion. The only slip coaches about which anything is now known are four brake thirds constructed between 1903 and 1905, which each held 48 third class passengers in two open compartments (one compartment presumably being for non-smokers). These were from a batch of seven, and were bogie vehicles 54 ft in length and 9 ft wide. The other three were not slip-fitted. There must have been other slip vehicles used on the L&YR at this time, since between 1893 and 1914 there were never fewer than six slips daily, and in some years there were eight. Of those built or adapted before 1903 nothing is known.

The London Brighton and South Coast Railway, which until the years when Earle Marsh was locomotive and carriage superintendent used (apart from Pullman cars) only arc-roofed passenger stock, employed only this type of carriage for slip vehicles, with a single exception, a six-wheeled brake composite coach used on the afternoon train from Victoria to Heathfield, which was slipped at Ashurst for Tunbridge Wells; this was elliptical-roofed. All LB&SCR slip coaches were single ended with a central end window.

I am indebted to Mr G.R. Weddell for the following information about slip vehicles on the London and South Western Railway:

Two slip brakes were built by the LSWR in 1896-1898. They were 48 ft long, with four passenger compartments, and a luggage compartment between them and the slip guard's compartment. In addition to rear windows in the end duckets there was a central window. These carriages were numbered 126 and 332; after several re-numberings they became SR 2722 and 2723. They were withdrawn in 1935 and 1937. Since there were at least four slips leaving Waterloo in the early evening at this time (*i.e. the turn of the century*) it seems there must have been other slip brakes built during the Adams regime, of which nothing is known - unless some brake vehicles from the 1860s continued in modified form.

Finally one may briefly mention the only slip coach built for the London and North Western Railway of which particulars survive. In 1913 this railway built a single double-ended slip coach, on four-wheeled bogies, 57 ft long, with two first and two third class compartments. It was unusual in having a raised look-out roof at either end, with a short ladder by each centre window up which the guard could climb to get an all-round view. By not having the usual duckets it was possible to build this coach to the full width of nine feet. One naturally wonders how the slip guard could operate all the necessary controls while standing on the ladder, or whether he had to descend in a hurry to do so.

Chapter Eight

Slip Coach Accidents

During the whole period when carriages were being slipped from passenger trains in Great Britain and Ireland only two serious accidents occurred, in both cases with only minor injuries to passengers, though on the second occasion two of the company's servants were seriously hurt. In each incident the portion that had just been slipped ran into the rear of the train from which it had been detached. That this should have happened only twice in the course of more than a century says much for the safety of the system, for during that time at least a million slips must have been made altogether. The human misunderstandings and errors that contributed to these two mishaps were also of a kind which present day methods of communication between driver and slip guard would have prevented.

The first was at Mark's Tey, on the Great Eastern Railway, on a winter evening, 29th December, 1906. The 5.30 pm from Liverpool Street to Ipswich, headed by a four-coupled locomotive (the type and number not being stated in the Board of Trade Report, but it was probably a Holden 2-4-0) and made up to 15 coaches, had carried a slip portion for many years, destined for Sudbury and Bury St Edmunds. The main train had eight six-wheelers, two bogie coaches and a four-wheeled bullion van; the four coaches of the slip portion were also six-wheelers. The night was misty when the train left the terminus, but not so much as to suggest that the slip should not be made. At Chelmsford, reached a few minutes late, the train made its only stop before Mark's Tey. Weather conditions had not noticeably deteriorated, and both footplate crew and guards were expecting the slip would be duly effected since no word to the contrary had been given them at Chelmsford.

However, out at Mark's Tey conditions *were* worsening, and by 6.35 pm the station master, Arthur Green, came to the conclusion that the mist had become too dense to allow the slip to be safely made. It was now too late to notify the driver and guards on the approaching train, so Green instructed the signalman to put the distant, home and starting signals at danger. It was presumed that the red signal lights would be visible and that no detonators need be set; there would in any case have been scarcely enough time in which to do this, the train being now only a few minutes away. The expectation was that the driver would brake his train as soon as he saw the distant signal, and stop at the home signal; he would then have been told to draw forward so that all the coaches were at the platform, and the slip portion would then have been detached. The fact of a brake application having been made before the distant signal had been reached would, it was assumed, have alerted the slip guard and caused him not to pull his slipping lever. The distant signal, it should be noted, was a tall one with an upper and lower arm, the latter being almost at eye-level so far as an observer on the train was concerned.

However, Harry Pizzey, the driver of the locomotive, did not catch sight of the lights on the distant signal until he had almost reached them. Supposing then that the slip had already been made, he did not make a sharp application of the train's brakes when he did at last see the red light on the lower semaphore arm, so that no indication was given to the slip guard, who, as a matter of fact, had not yet made the slip, since he had not seen, or said he had not seen the distant signal light at all, though he claimed when giving evidence that he had been taking extra precautions, looking out from his compartment window all the way from Chelmsford. When the train went beneath an overbridge, which slip guard George Bonner knew to be a little way beyond the distant signal, he slipped his portion, believing it to be perfectly safe to do so. He had, he thought, enough braking power in his hand brake as well as the extra power in his Westinghouse brake cylinders which he meant to use in the final run up to the platform. (Actually it was against the regulations to do this except in an emergency. One wonders if this were a rule more honoured then in the breach rather than the observance.)

The driver meanwhile, having done no more than shut off steam when he saw the distant signal at red, braked further when he saw that the home signal was also against him, but was still moving when the train reached the platform end. The foreman porter, standing there, observed that the train was not its usual complete length, realised that the slip *had* been made, and shouted to the signalman to lower the starting signal. This was done, but before the driver could observe this he had already decided to pull forward past that signal to a point where he believed it would be safe to stop, leaving (as he supposed) enough platform room behind his last carriage for the slip portion to draw in to its usual stopping-place. However, he misjudged the distance; the rear of his train was still at the further end of the platform when he finally halted. A quarter of a minute later the slip portion, travelling at a reduced speed whose rate no one could agree about, collided with the back of the main train. The impact was sufficient to damage the six rear vehicles of the main train and all four in the slip portion. Thirty-four people were injured, none seriously.

The Inspecting Officer for the Board of Trade, Colonel P.G. von Donop, came to the conclusion that the slip guard, George Bonner, had been chiefly responsible for the accident, but that the driver, Harry Pizzey, had also in some measure contributed to it. Had the latter done what was appropriate when he saw the distant signal at danger, and immediately applied the Westinghouse brake throughout the train, the slip guard would have known it was unsafe to slip. (This was true, but driver Pizzey had, for reasons given above, deliberately not immediately applied his brakes, since he thought that the slip had already been made. But he should not have assumed this, for he had seen no sign from the slip guard, through the waving of a red lamp, that this had happened. Indeed, he had not even looked for this sign, thinking, probably correctly, that he could not have seen it through the mist.)

Von Donop also criticised Pizzey for incorrectly judging how far in advance of the starting signal he should have brought his train to a stand. Another couple of hundred yards, and the accident would not have happened unless Bonner had made the further mistake of aiming to halt the slip portion beyond the usual place - as indeed he might have done, for the slip had been made beyond the usual place of detachment.

It was Bonner, however, on whom the chief blame rested. In the words of the Report:

> [The guard] himself admits that when he reached the overbridge-he knew where he was, and he recognised that he had passed the distant signal without seeing it; under those circumstances it was his duty to have treated the signal as a danger signal, and consequently not to have made the slip. He was doubtless misled by the fact of the driver not having checked the speed of the train, but that did not justify him in neglecting to carry out his own instructions; he could either have attracted the driver's attention by the application of the automatic brake, in which case the whole train would doubtless have been brought to a stand, or he could have allowed the slip portion to be taken forward to the next station. It is to Bonner's error in slipping the carriages when he did that the accident must be mainly attributed.
>
> When approaching the station, also, Bonner does not appear to have adhered to the regulations. He states that when he reached the platform he was going at a speed of about 15 miles an hour, and that he felt he could stop the vehicles in their usual place by the application of the Westinghouse brake. It is evident therefore that Bonner intended to make use of that brake . . . whilst Rule No. 7 (e) . . . states that except in cases of emergency the continuous brake must not be used by the slip guard after slipping. Bonner should therefore have entered the station at a speed at which he could have stopped his carriages by the application of the hand-brake alone. Had he adhered to this rule, the speed at the time of the collision would certainly not have been as great as it actually was.*

Von Donop also doubted Bonner's statement that he could not see the tail lamp at the rear of the main train, which according to the evidence was burning brightly at the time. The foreman porter on the platform had seen the lights of the approaching slip coach when it was as much as 150 yards away. Allowing for the fact that the brake van windows were frozen, even so Bonner, he felt, ought to have observed the tail lamp of the train in time to have prevented a collision.

Von Donop had the last word, and it is difficult to fault his conclusions. A few comments, however, may not be out of place. One would think that Bonner's very familiarity with this particular slip at this particular place may, paradoxically, have been contributory to the accident. On this single occasion, out of hundreds, something unusual happened. In all walks of life rules tend in practice to be modified, and chances are taken or corners cut. Car drivers modify what the Highway Code tells them most times they drive. Bonner probably felt 99.9 per cent sure that the distant signal he had not seen was at 'all clear', for it always had been. As to his statement that he had not seen the rear light of the main train, which von Donop took leave to doubt, it is a fact of psychology that one tends not to see what one does not expect to see. He had good reasons not to cause the train to halt at Mark's Tey; it was already running late, and a stop to detach the carriages would have added several minutes to its lateness. The driver had not braked the train, so clearly that unobserved distant signal *must* have shown green, not red. Common sense had to decide what should be done in a situation the regulations did not specifically provide for - a combination of fog and freezing cold which made one important rule impossible of observance: the injunction to show a green light to the driver after

---

* *Board of Trade Report on Accident at Mark's Tey, 29/12/1906*: P.G. von Donop: pp. 61-62.

the slip had been made, or a red one if it had not been made.

In regard to Bonner's intention to use the Westinghouse brake to bring about the final deceleration at the station platform, one rather suspects that here was a rule that was regularly disregarded when this seemed advisable to the man on the spot. So long as he did not use up all the compressed air in the slip vehicle's reservoir, at such a late point in the coach's run in, no risk would be involved, and the company's regulations might well have recognised this, and allowed this brake to be used from the platform end onwards. Particularly this might have been helpful when the slip portion was a large one (as on the Mark's Tey slip) with hand brakes usable only on the slip carriage itself. The GWR did allow the use of the vacuum brake in this way in later days, providing its slip vehicles with additional vacuum reservoirs to allow up to three automatic brake applications while the slip was coming in.

One also suspects that Bonner may have been a tired man. At the time of the accident he had been on duty for 11 hours, with only two short breaks in which to relax. He had also been working until 10.15 the previous evening. A little over nine hours is not a long while, after a full day, in which to go home, have a meal, get some sleep, rise and return to work. Those were days when railway companies did not give much thought to ensuring that their employees were in a sufficiently rested state to perform their duties to their own and others' safety. One remembers the well-known oil painting which hangs in the Railwaymen's Union (RMT) headquarters in London: the signalman clutching a lever and staring forward with eyes wearied from too long a spell of duty. Bonner, who doubtless lost his job in consequence of the accident, was even more a victim of the event than the passengers with their bumps and bruises. The moral is plain, and has later been increasingly acted upon: eliminate the human element as far as possible and install automatic devices to supplement or replace human vigilance.

The other serious accident involving a slip coach occurred on what was one of the more prestigious trains on the former Great Central system, which provided an evening express service to Sheffield and Bradford that competed well with the corresponding evening service on the former Midland system. It was one of the Central Section of the LNER's more difficult assignments, since in addition to the main portion for Bradford it also conveyed a coach for Barnsley and, at the time when the accident occurred, two slip carriages as well, detached respectively at Finmere and Woodford.* For the first 58 miles of its journey, therefore, it was an eight-coach train made up of heavy stock which included a restaurant car. It took the GW&LNE Joint Line from Northolt Junction to Ashendon Junction in order to avoid the evening congestion on the Metropolitan & LNE route; the former, while not as severely graded as the latter, was 4½ miles longer and had some hampering service slacks, so was on balance no easier. For the 107.9 miles from Marylebone to Leicester 114 minutes were allowed. Haulage was regularly entrusted to a four-coupled ex-GCR Robinson 'Atlantic'.

All things considered, it was one of the most tightly-timed trains on the LNER system, and the locomotive allotted, which worked southwards from Leicester earlier in the day, was always given special treatment during its turn-round

---

* See Chapter Four for further information about these two slips.

period to help it to face the rigours of the evening run. The two slip coaches detached at Finmere and Woodford were the two built for the GCR during 1911-1912, mentioned in the previous chapter. At the end of each was a small brake compartment housing the slipping gear. By 1923, when they passed into LNER ownership, the mechanical arrangements had been somewhat altered; vacuum reservoirs had now been fitted to allow the guard to use the vacuum brake as well as the hand brake. In other respects, apart from changes in livery, titling and numbering, the two coaches were as when first built.

On the evening of Thursday 19th December, 1935 the 6.20 pm left Marylebone with the usual eight coaches, hauled by No. 6068, driven by Ernest Cawkwell of Leicester Shed. This engine, a 4-4-2, one of Robinson's 'Jersey Lilies', was now fully 30 years old, but had been modified in 1914 to receive a superheated boiler and rather larger cylinders. On a cold winter evening, when a good deal of the steam produced in the boiler had to be diverted to heat the carriages, the 290-ton train posed a problem on this fast schedule, and by the time the Finmere coach was slipped some minutes had already been lost. As Woodford was approached, therefore, the engine was going 'all out' to try if possible to recover time, and the amount of smoke and steam it was expelling from its chimney was a factor in increasing the amount of damage that was to ensue, as will be seen below.

The usual point of slipping was a disused signal box a little to the south of Woodford, and the slip guard, Charles Robertson, duly effected the slip at this point, adhering carefully to all the regulations. The main train began, as expected, to draw away from the slip coach, and Robertson signalled to the driver that the slip had been made by waving his green lamp out of the window. Gradually the tail light of the main train diminished in the distance.

However, something had gone wrong, of which Robertson was quite unaware. The sealing of the brake pipes, preparatory to loosening the coupling, was effected by pulling a cord, and when he did this, while the slip coach's pipe was effectively sealed, that on the rear coach of the main train began to leak. Vacuum was lost and the main train's brakes began to be applied. Why this was happening the driver could not know, but he may well have thought that it was a sign from Robertson to say that for some reason the slip had not been made. He certainly did think this for another reason; he had not seen Robertson's green light signal when he looked back along the train. Drifting steam from the engine had obscured it. So when his train had been brought to a halt through the operation of the continuous brake he had no idea that the already-slipped coach was following behind.

Of this brake-fault the slip guard was completely unaware. Had it still been daylight he would have seen the whole train ahead of him. Had it not been for the drifting steam he could have seen its tail light in the darkness. Furthermore, this steam hung around behind the main train the more densely because the approach to Woodford was through a cutting. So Robertson was not aware that the express had stopped until it was too late to avert a collision. His carriage struck the rear of the main train at about 20 mph and telescoped into it. Both he and the guard of the main train, Richard Bonnett, were badly hurt; 11 passengers also received minor injuries.

The Official Report on the accident by the Ministry of Transport's Inspecting Officer, Lieutenant Colonel E. Woodhouse, put the blame not on any of the company's servants but squarely on the shoulders of the company itself. Exactly why the train's brake pipe had not closed could not be determined, but two alternative explanations were put forward. The first was that when Robinson had pulled the cord to close the brake cock the latter's lever had not come round by the full 90 degrees; subsequently when falling back it had struck a projection from the coach to which it was attached and had been knocked partly open again. The alternative was that there had been too great a tension between the brake pipe hoses and that these had come apart too quickly; the sudden jerk when the pipes separated had caused the cock on the main train to re-open.

It was evident to the Inspecting Officer that the company was not using the best possible equipment. On the GWR an improved type of brake-pipe cock was then in use, in which this sort of malfunctioning could not have occurred. He suggested that the LNER authorities should adopt the GWR method in place of their own. On the former Great Eastern section this improved method was already being used. However, the LNER had already decided on a more drastic solution altogether - to discontinue slipping on the Central section. Consequently, from February 1936 onwards the 6.20 pm from Marylebone made brief stops at both Finmere and Woodford, and no longer conveyed a through carriage to Stratford-upon-Avon. Five minutes only were added to the train's schedule between London and Leicester, the final stage from Woodford being covered at an average of 60 mph. The short time addition would not in itself have been enough for the making of two extra one-minute stops had the same engine provision been continued, but the ancient and over-worked Robinson 'Atlantics' were soon taken off this duty and newer 'B17' 4-6-0s of Gresley's design, considerably more powerful, replaced them. Thus timekeeping, if no easier, was at least no harder than before.

Appendix One

An Unofficial Slip
Working in 1838

Canon R.B. Fellows, to whose researches I have been much indebted while preparing this book, contributed an article in *The Locomotive* of 15th January, 1944, about what must surely have been the first occasion when a vehicle of any sort was slipped from a moving train. It was an entirely unofficial operation and one fraught with some danger. The perpetrator was Herbert Spencer, in later years the well-known Victorian agnostic philosopher but then as a young man working as an employee of the London and Birmingham Railway. The date was during September 1838; the railway had not yet been completely opened and Spencer had been told to make a survey of the new station at Wolverton. He completed this in time to get the last train back towards London, which was due to halt at Watford and then run non-stop. He then commandeered a truck to be attached to the train, but had to make do with one having no brake. Travelling in the train as far as Watford, he then transferred himself to the truck intending to detach its coupling when passing through Harrow so that it would drop back behind the train and, he hoped, come to rest near Wembley, where his lodgings were.

However, after the uncoupling, the truck continued to remain close behind the train; the down gradient of 1 in 330 ensured that the friction in the wheel bearings was insufficient to bring about quick deceleration. So the vehicle swept on past Wembley and only started to slow down when the 1 in 330 gave place to level track near Brent. Not far ahead there was a level crossing whose gates, Spencer knew, would be closed against him. Fortunately the truck drew to a stand before the gates were reached. Spencer then aroused the crossing gate keeper and the two men managed to manhandle the truck back along the line to a siding near Brent, where it was diverted off the main line, leaving the latter clear for trains to pass, and walked back to his lodgings.

Appendix Two

Slips Made from the 'Cornish Riviera Express'

As this, the Great Western Railway's 'flagship' train, was the most famous one in Britain to carry slip portions, some account of its use of slip carriages, as this varied through the years, would not seem out of place. The train first began to run as a non-stop service to Plymouth, continuing to Penzance, as a summer-only service, without any distinguishing name. It received much publicity, since no other train in the country ran without a stop for over 200 miles - and in this case, since it had to travel by way of Swindon and Bristol, the non-stop journey was not much short of 250 miles. It was not at first a heavy train, being composed of five clerestory compartment coaches and a restaurant car; it was hauled by a 'City' 4-4-0 and allowed four hours 25 minutes for its run to Plymouth. Much was made of it in the Railway press at the time, and a public competition held to suggest a suitable name for it, which resulted in its being entitled 'The Cornish Riviera Express'.

No slips were made from it while it was taking the route through Bristol, but in 1906 the new express route to the west by way of Castle Cary was completed, and the Cornish Riviera Express followed it, becoming 20 minutes faster to Plymouth over a route 20 miles shorter. Haulage was now entrusted to six-coupled locomotives, and their extra power permitted the addition of slip portions for Westbury (which continued to Weymouth) and for Exeter (which went on to Torquay). In 1907 a slip portion was added for Taunton, so that the load became nine or ten coaches for the first 95 miles of its journey. The short clerestoried coaches originally used now gave place to longer and more commodious ones, which made the whole train heavier. Haulage was now entrusted to 4-cylinder 4-6-0 'Stars'. This pattern continued for several years, until the exigencies of World War I resulted in the drastic contraction of all train services and the suspension of all slip coach services. The schedule during this pre-War period was as follows: Paddington, depart 10.30 am, slip made at Westbury, 12.07 pm; slip made at Taunton, 1.00 pm; slip made at Exeter, 1.30 pm; Plymouth, arrive 2.37 pm.

Eight months after the end of the War the 'Cornish Riviera Express' returned, with slips at Taunton and Exeter, and the following October the Westbury slip also returned, together with the former schedule. Two years later it had become a 400-ton train out of Paddington, slipping portions at Westbury (for Weymouth), Taunton (for Ilfracombe and Minehead) and Exeter (for Torquay). Haulage was still entrusted to 4-6-0s of the 'Star' class, but in 1923 there appeared the more powerful 'Castles'; the load now frequently mounted to 14 coaches out of Paddington, with two being detached at each slipping place. From 1927 the even more powerful 'Kings' were employed. In 1929 three special slip coaches were built specially for use on this train.

During the early 1930s the pattern continued as in 1927. In 1935, however, there were three changes. One was the provision of new coaching stock, with end doors only, for the main part of the train; another was the completion (in 1933) of a cut-off line which enabled through trains to avoid Westbury station, with its curve; a third was the acceleration of the train to reach Plymouth in the even four hours. The slips at Taunton and Exeter were now discontinued, these places being served by a following train, so that only the one at Westbury remained - and this was not slipped at the same place as before, but rather further back, so that the coaches could come to rest before Heywood Road Junction signal box, from which, after the points had been moved, a shunting engine could take them into Westbury platform. Hence, though the whole train was faster to Plymouth, it was three minutes slower to Westbury. This pattern, of a slip at Westbury only, continued to be the pattern until the outbreak of World War II, when all slips were discontinued for the duration.

After the War slipping returned, but only on the GWR and (later) the Western Region of British Railways. The 'Cornish Riviera Express' returned, though at first on a slower timing, and the single slip at Westbury was again made. By the late 1950s another change had occurred: steam haulage had given place to diesel haulage, with 2,200 hp diesel-hydraulic 'Warships' replacing the 'Kings'. Soon afterwards the Westbury slip was discontinued, the last one being made on 12th September, 1959.

Appendix Three

G.W.T. Daniel's Slip-Coach Table

In an article about Slip Coach Services in the July 1935 *Railway Magazine* Mr Daniel included a very informative table which seems worth reproducing here. It is not completely comprehensive of Slip Coach history, since when he was writing this still had 25 years more to run, but it does illustrate the pattern of the rise and fall of this phenomenon over three-quarters of a century.

The last four sections deal with Irish lines; the slips shown in the last two columns for 'GSWR/MGWR' were actually made when both these railways had been merged into the Great Southern Railway of Ireland. Similarly, all those in the 1924 column should be shown as either LMS, LNER, GWR or SR.

Railway	Slips Commenced	Slips Given Up	No. of Places	Greatest Number in a Year	Totals										Still left
					1875	1880	1885	1890	1895	1900	1908	1914	1918	1924	1934
Total	—	—	—	—	58	88	92	122	127	129	178	200	17	93	29
G.W. & L.N.W. Jt.	1868	1894	1	2 in 1880	—	2	2	1	—	—	—	—	—	—	—
G.W.R.	Dec., 1858	—	43	79 in 1908	25	32	26	30	42	49	79	72	—	47	23
S.E.R.	July, 1860	July, 1924	11	11 in 1863–65	4	3	3	3	3	1	2	3	—	3	—
L.C.D.R.	Dec., 1872	July, 1926	6	5 in 1896, &c.	3	3	3	4	3	4	3	6	—	7	—
L.B.S.C.	Summer, 1858	Apr., 1932	11	27 in 1914	3	7	8	9	9	9	14	27	2	21	—
L.S.W.R.	March, 1887	May, 1902	—	4 in 1896, &c.	—	—	—	2	3	4	—	—	—	—	—
L.N.W.R.	March, 1869	Dec., 1916	11	18 in 1914–15 (+ 1 news-paper)	2	1	1	1	—	9	16	18	—	—	—
M.R.	July, 1366	Dec., 1916	26	25 in 1888	—	—	—	19	17	5	13	21	—	—	—
Furness Rly.	July, 1887	Dec., 1916	5	7 in 1891	—	—	—	4	5	3	2	1	—	—	—
L.Y.R.	Oct., 1886	Oct., 1926	7	8 in 1899, &c.	—	—	—	5	6	8	7	7	5	6	—
Caledonian	Jan., 1904	Dec., 1916	9	14 in 1911	—	—	—	—	—	—	12	12	—	—	—
G.S.W.R.	June, 1898	Sep., 1901	1	1 in 1899, &c.	—	—	—	—	—	1	—	—	—	—	—
G.N.R.	Oct., 1864	Dec., 1916	12	30 in 1883	15	27	27	17	9	6	1	1	—	—	—
G.E.R.	June, 1872	—	15	25 in 1904	2	9	17	18	20	23	16	18	—	3	2*
M.S.L.–G.C.	May, 1886	—	11	11 in 1894	—	—	—	6	7	1	2	4	—	2	—
N.E.R.	Jan., 1871	1905	3	3	1	1	1	1	1	1	—	—	—	—	—
N.B.R.	May, 1870	May, 1894	5	3	3	3	3	2	—	—	—	—	—	—	—
Eskdale	July, 1921	1924	1	1	—	—	—	—	—	—	—	—	—	—	—
G.S.W.R.	June, 1901	—	7	9	—	—	—	—	—	—	8	8	7	—	1
M.G.W.R.	1909	July, 1928	1	2	—	—	—	—	—	—	—	1	2	1	—
B. & N.C. (N.C.C.)	July, 1895	Sep., 1916	4	4	—	—	—	—	2	2	1	1	—	—	1†
G.N. (I.)	August, 1896	—	7	3	—	—	—	—	—	3	2	—	1	2	—
B. & C.D.	Nov., 1902	Apr., 1918	1	1	—	—	—	—	—	1‡	1‡	1‡	—	—	

* 1 in Summer   † In Summer   ‡ Saturday

Appendix Four

Was the South Eastern Railway actually the first to slip coaches?

Although the Brighton Line has usually been credited with inaugurating the practice of slipping carriages from moving trains, it is just possible that the South Eastern Railway was the first in the field. That railway's January 1858 timetable included a note regarding the 4.25 pm from Charing Cross to Hastings, saying that it 'leaves London passengers at Penshurst, Etchingham and Battle: *train does not stop at Etchingham*'. A similar note appears regarding the 4.30 pm down, relating to Godstone. How could a train leave passengers at a station without stopping there, unless it slipped a coach or coaches?

One way of explaining this would be to assume that the company was not so much giving information about the behaviour of the train, but indicating that while it carried passengers *to* a particular station, it did not undertake to carry them *from* that station; it was the equivalent of stops to set down only. Nothing is said about the provision of a special coach for passengers to either place.

In the case of the LB&SCR's slip at Haywards Heath, here two trains had been combined into one for something like half the second train's journey; and the use of a slip portion represented a definite economy. It is difficult to see what economies might have been effected in the case of the putative slips at Etchingham and Godstone, which were, then, quite small places where probably only a few passengers would have alighted. Neither station served a branch line, as did Haywards Heath. It might have been convenient for a single carriage to have been detached at either place, and this could have been done if the train stopped momentarily outside the station. To have slipped it, however, would have meant the building of a special vehicle, or the adaptation of an existing one, and the employment of a special slip guard.

Further evidence is needed to be sure, one way or the other, such as a set of working instructions issued by the South Eastern Railway, or definite information about the provision of a specially- made slip carriage. If full details should still exist about early coach construction at Bricklayer's Arms or Ashford, and if nothing at all is said in them about the making of special vehicles for slipping (there would have had to be at least two) the matter could then be regarded as settled.

Appendix Five

Cord communication on slip coaches prior to automatic braking

In the days before the continuous automatic braking of trains became the rule on all passenger services, some form of communication between passengers and the driver and guard of the train was required. The usual device was a continuous cord, running outside and above the windows of the train and reaching to the locomotive, where it could sound an alarm, such as striking a bell or a gong. In October 1883 the Great Western Railway issued a set of six rules, by which this precaution could be extended to slip coaches. According to Canon R.B. Fellows, in an article in the *Railway Magazine* for November 1936, the rules

> . . . gave the following directions for arrangements whereby passengers could communicate with the slip guard; the usual wheel and bell must be provided in the brake compartment of the slip coach; the cord must be fixed to the rear of the slip coach (or of the last coach of a slip set), be carried along the coach and the other end be attached to the wheel in the guard's compartment of the slip. To enable the slip guard to communicate with the guard of the main train, the rules stated that a short cord must be fastened to the cord on the last vehicle of the main train, which must be passed through a tube provided in the guard's compartment, so that, if required, the slip guard could pull it and thus communicate with the guard and driver of the train; the end of this cord must be loose so that it might run out when the slip coach separated from the train.
>   The rules stated that if there were two sets of slips the second set must be treated exactly like the first; thus the guard in the second set would be able to ring to the guard of the first set, who would then ring to the guard and driver of the main train and so stop the train. The rules added that 'the small pieces of cord must be taken care of by the guard of the main train or the guard of the first set of slip coaches, as the case may be, and be brought back to the starting station to be used the next day.'

The care taken to preserve the 'small pieces of cord' is perhaps indicative of a 19th century desire for economy in small things, taking care of the pence so that the pounds would take care of themselves. One is not told how they were attached to the longer cord which ran the length of the train. Probably they were not knotted together but joined by a pair of hooks.

Canon Fellows inquired at the end of his article how the London Brighton and South Coast Railway coped with this problem, since they had their own special system of communication invented by Stroudley. A former signalman supplied the answer the following month.

> The slip guard controlled the same equipment as the other guards and the enginemen, and could give the same bell signals. The code used on the Brighton Line was: one ring 'All right'; two rings 'Danger; stop the train'; and three rings 'Prepare for slipping carriages at speed. Continuous ringing, of course, meant that a passenger had operated the communication from a compartment. On approaching a slip station the driver, if the distant signal was off, gave three rings, and the slip guard replied. The latter then exchanged hand signals with the train guard, and the slip was made. The train guard then gave one ring, which the driver acknowledged, signifying that the slip had been properly effected. Strict rules governed the testing of this equipment before the train started, signals being exchanged between the engine and the slip guard, or guards. Unless everything was in perfect order slipping was not allowed. If engines were changed on the way, for any reason, the testing had to be gone through again.

Whereas on the GWR the method of communication was entirely mechanical and could be relatively slow in operation, especially if there were two slip portions, on the LB&SCR it was electrical and operated immediately. One can well understand why the latter company was so anxious to have a quick and reliable system of passenger-guard-driver communication, for it was on one of its trains that a passenger had been murdered in a compartment during the passage of a tunnel.

Appendix Six

Early slips on the
London and South Western Railway

Most railways, if they experimented with slipping but did not continue it, adopted and then discarded it just the once. The London and South Western, however, did so twice, at first in a small way, later more considerably. I have not been able to find out much about the earlier period. Mr G.R. Weddell, however, contributes the following information:

On the LSWR in the 1860s, since coupling hooks were bolted on to the drawbar, any brake vehicle could have its coupler replaced by a slipping one easily. This latter had a sleeve over a catch on a collar acting as a coupler, and this was drawn free by the slip guard pulling a cord. There is some evidence that the coupling hook was unbolted, probably at the slipping station and returned to Waterloo, a normal hook being bolted to the drawbar in its place. The last coach of the main train showed a green light as well as a red one.

If the special slip-coupling hooks were indeed unbolted in this manner, and returned to the terminus to be fixed to another brake vehicle, then clearly the latter had to be one that was fitted with an end window so that the guard could see clearly what he was doing. It seems that all early LSWR brake vehicles were thus provided.

Appendix Seven

The Travelling Post Office Slip Van used on the GWR Ocean Mails' train

The origin of the GWR 'Ocean Mails' service was the calling of a German transatlantic liner off Plymouth, *en route* for Germany, to disembark passengers and mails from America. The former were taken to London by the LSWR, the mails to Paddington by the GWR, via Bristol, a stop being made here to detach two vans which were then taken on to Birmingham and the Midlands. This stop was replaced by a slip in 1905, at Pylle Hill Junction, the junction for the loop line which avoided Temple Meads station, Bristol, in order to delay the London-bound mails as little as possible. A special Post Office slip van was ordered in 1904 and completed in January 1905. According to Michael Harris, it was

> . . . originally built with gangways at both ends, with the usual guard's slip compartment, it was later modified with a side gangway at one end only, and a lavatory was installed. It also had a wired glass top to the roof, a feature followed in the 1905 TPO stock, and . . . had three recessed doors on each side, as against sliding doors . . . No. 537 lost its slip apparatus about 1917, but retained the window at one end, and in the 1940s became non-corridor.[*]

The service it provided became, of course, unnecessary in August 1914, when German ships of all kinds ceased to call at British ports. Its usefulness for slipping then vanished.

The van is described by Michael Harris, in his complete list of GWR coaches built between 1890 and 1954 as a 'sorting van', but this is incorrect. It was a 'stowage van'. A plan of it appears on page 10 of J.H. Russell's book *Great Western Coaches: 1903-1948*, as later modified with a gangway at one end only, which was to one side, not central. It was lettered 'OCEAN MAILS' in large letters below the waist. Originally it had three double doors on the near side and only one on the off side, but two more were later added to the latter. These were outwardly-hinged, not sliding doors, and permitted the belt conveyers to transfer mailbags straight from the tender vessel which had brought them from the ship. The van was 68 ft long and 9½ ft wide, and foreshadowed the later 'Dreadnought' stock in its construction.

---

[*] M. Harris: *Great Western Coaches, 1890-1954*: p. 124.

Appendix Eight

Did the Midland Railway operate vestibuled slip coaches?

There can be no doubt that this railway built such coaches; what is not certain is whether they were actually slipped from restaurant car trains as envisaged.

In his paper, read before members of the Railway Club in October 1941, Canon Fellows, after referring to the LNWR slip coaches used in 1914 between Euston and Coventry, went on:

Is this a unique example of detaching a vestibuled slip coach, or did the Midland Railway anticipate it in 1910 or 1911? This railway certainly intended to slip a somewhat similar coach, and issued in the Appendix to the Working Timetable of 1911 elaborate instructions. I can find no reference in any contemporary paper or magazine to what would have been a novelty, and the LNWR's Coventry slip in 1914 is certainly treated as a novelty by the *Railway Magazine*. It seems unlikely that, if the Midland Railway slips had been made and were still in operation in 1914, that they should not have been mentioned in this connection. The Midland Company's proposal of 1910 or 1911, if actually put into practice, seems to me to have been in contravention of the Regulation of Railways Act, 1889, as to the use of the continuous brake on passenger trains, and certainly to have been attended with some danger.

The instructions in the Appendix to the Working Timetable of June 1911 regarding the continuous brake are as follows: '*Vacuum Brake and Ordinary Screw Coupling*: The vacuum brake and ordinary screw coupling must be in use between the slip carriage and main train until the last stopping station prior to slipping is reached.

'*Adjusting of Slip Apparatus and release of Vacuum Brake on Slip Portion*: At the last stopping place prior to slipping the vacuum pipes between the slip carriage and the main train must be separated and placed on the plugs, and care must be taken that the vacuum brake on the slip portion is released by pulling the wire underneath the slip carriage.* The slip coupling must then be adjusted in the ordinary way.

'*Hand brake*: A specially powerful hand brake is provided on slip corridor carriages, which operates on all eight wheels.

'*Means of Communication between Passengers and Guard*: When a slip corridor carriage is running under slip regulations, the passengers will be unable to apply the brake by means of the chain communication, but when the latter is used a bell will be rung in the guard's compartment. When the bell rings the slip guard must at once proceed along the slip corridor, ascertain the cause for which the chain has been pulled, and if desirable to stop the train go through the gangway into the next carriage and apply the vacuum brake. Special care must be taken that the bell is properly wound up.'

It will be noticed from the above instructions, firstly, that though the station for slipping may be many miles distant from the previous stopping station, during the whole of that distance neither the driver nor any guard on the train could apply the continuous brake to the last carriage, the slip coach, in case of an emergency, nor could the guard in the slip van apply the continuous brake at all. Secondly, after the slip coach has been detached the slip guard would have no automatic vacuum brake in reserve to stop the slip coach in case of an emergency. The seriousness of this was no doubt realised by the company and minimised to some extent by the specially powerful hand brake fitted to this type of coach, and by an instruction that 'if the passengers for the slip carriage are in excess of what the coach will accommodate, the train must be stopped'. Only one coach was to be slipped.

The common form of the Regulations issued in August 1892 contained a clause that 'the continuous brake must be capable of being applied to every vehicle of the train, whether carrying passengers or not. However, some exceptions were allowed, and a proportion of vehicles, unbraked but fitted with continuous brake pipe connections, was permitted. The last vehicle was, however, to be fitted with the continuous brake for application to its wheels, 'provided, however, that where necessary to avoid delay in working, one vehicle only, not fitted with the continuous brake used by the Company, may be placed in the rear of the train . . .'

---

* 'Released' here sounds ambiguous, but obviously it does not mean the release of air into the vacuum chamber, which would apply the brakes; what is released from operation is the whole braking system, so that the vacuum reservoirs remain unopened and unopenable.

Now, until 1911, *no* slip coach was *not* thus fitted on any railway, so, strictly interpreted, the permissive conclusion could not have applied to any existing coach. The MR, it seems, were envisaging a departure from the existing regulations, hoping that their alternative plan, to fit the proposed corridor slip coaches with hand braking on all eight wheels, would be approved instead. The company's rules allowed a passenger in a corridor slip coach to operate the alarm cord, but if this were done after the last stopping station before the slip it would not have applied the continuous brake but instead have operated a bell in the slip guard's compartment. The slip coach guard would then have gone to see what was wrong, and if he judged it necessary to halt the train he would have gone back through his own compartment and the vestibule to the last coach of the parent train and applied the continuous brake there. However, suppose that the alarm cord were pulled at the moment of slipping or after. It was vitally necessary then for the slip guard to remain at his controls. What was he to do if he heard the alarm bell? How could he safely leave his controls while the slip carriage was in motion. Robbery or murder might be happening in one of the compartments behind him, but if he left his controls the lives of all the passengers were at risk. This was a possible event the MR seems to have overlooked, and perhaps the Board of Trade had to point it out.

Canon Fellows seems to have been sceptical as to whether the MR really did build such coaches, but in fact they built five in 1911.[*] Each was double-ended, with a central vestibule-attachment at each end to the left of which was a window that gave the slip guard his necessary view forwards. In the plans a hand brake wheel is shown in each compartment. The question of whether these carriages were ever used as slip coaches in restaurant car trains as intended cannot be answered without further evidence. They were certainly used in ordinary service, for a photograph exists of one of them immediately behind the tender of a Midland & South Western Junction locomotive on a through train from Cheltenham, standing at the platform at Andover. Canon Fellows ends his remarks by saying: 'The Railway Department of the Ministry of Transport, though aware of the LNWR's corridor slips of 1914, have no knowledge of a Midland slip of a similar kind.'

So for three reasons, (1) the absence of any evidence that such a slip service actually operated, (2) the fact that, used as proposed, it would have contravened the Board of Trade's regulations, and (3) the Ministry of Transport's statement that they knew nothing of such a service, it seems reasonable to assume that these vehicles were never employed in the intended manner.

---

[*] R.E. Lacy & G. Dow: *Midland Railway Carriages*, Vol. II: p. 334.

Appendix Nine

Slips made on the
Ravenglass and Eskdale Railway

With some hesitation I include these among the more important ones made from trains on standard gauge railways. Rather than as an economically beneficial public service, they were made as an additional tourist attraction on 'the Smallest Public Railway in the World'. Thus they ensured the RE&R took its place in the railway annals alongside the Great Western Railway, when Sir Aubrey Brocklebank was a Director of both companies!

During the summer services between 1921 and 1924 vehicles one or more of the 4-wheeled vehicles were slipped from eastbound trains at Irton Road. The 11.15 am was a non-stop run which thus made connections with the 'Red Runner' charabanc tours run by local operators to Wsatwater. According to G.W.T. Daniel 'this operation was performed with elemental simplicity by leaning out of the hindmost car in the main train and pulling the pin out of the coupling by which the rear car was attached'.* The main train carried red head and tail boards to indicate to trains passing in the other direction that another 'train' was following, and the slipped portion carried white head and tail boards to indicate it was complete and the line was clear behind in accordance with the complex working timetable of the time.

In a private letter Mr R.W. Kidner also adds: 'On 9/10th July, 1983 one coach was slipped four times each day at Irton Road station'. These were from non-stop trains proceeding up the valley during a special Enthusiast weekend, under regulations approved by the Railway Inspectorate. Similar workings have occurred as recently as the Narrow Gauge Railway Staff Gathering on 26th October, 1996, and have all the dramatic flavour of the main line slip coach workings which ceased in September 1960 at Bicester.

A carriage is slipped from the rear of a Ravenglass & Eskdale train at Muncaster Mill on 14th October, 1995.   *Ann Edwards*

* Article in *Railway Magazine*, July 1935, p. 15.

Appendix Ten

Returning slip vehicles to their bases

One of the disadvantages of the system of slipping coaches was that this kind of service could only operate in one direction. Usually, if such a coach or portion went from station A to station C, being slipped *en route* at B, it was afterwards marshalled in a particular train going from C to A and served as an ordinary passenger coach or group of coaches. Sometimes its movements were more complicated; for example, the Mark's Tey slip portion had to be divided before returning to Liverpool Street. In a letter to the author Mr R.W. Kidner wrote:

> The slip coach only had a vestibule connection at the non-brake end, while the last coach of the main portion had one only at the end away from the slip. In order that there should be no blank corridors on the up trains, the main train carriage with the blank end returned as the first coach of the 7 am from Clacton the next morning, and the slip coach and its trailer were formed as the first two coaches of the 9.55 am from Clacton after their arrival at Mark's Tey, having left Cambridge at 8.38.

In other words, the Mark's Tey slip portion, having reached its first intended destination at Bury St Edmunds, was then taken on to Cambridge by way of Ely, and returned the next day, its coaches retracing their path and being attached to the front of a train from Clacton, reaching Liverpool Street in time to be slipped again the same evening.

Another possibility was to slip a double-ended slip coach at a station B some distance from the starting point A, take it further on to station C by a later train, and then attach it to an up train to be slipped at station D *en route* for A. Thus its usefulness as a slip vehicle was increased. As mentioned in Chapter Three, too, a coach might be slipped twice without reversal, being detached from one train, then attached to another and slipped a second time from that train.

It is obvious that if it were to be used to greatest advantage a slip coach needed to be used daily. If slipped a long way from its base it might be more economical to send it straight back by the next available train even if the latter were a parcels train carrying no passengers. With slips made a very long way from their base, even this might not be feasible - the Carmarthen slip for Aberystwyth on the GWR and the Rugeley slip for Welshpool on the LNWR being cases in point; then there would have been no alternative to using a pair of slip coaches which took turns on alternate days.